CALVINISM

NONE DARE
CALL IT HERESY

CALVINISM
NONE DARE
CALL IT HERESY

Spotlight on the Life
and Teachings of
JOHN CALVIN

BOB KIRKLAND D.D.

LIGHTHOUSE TRAILS PUBLISHING
EUREKA, MONTANA

Calvinism: None Dare Call It Heresy
© 2018 Bob Kirkland D. D.
2nd Edition
By Lighthouse Trails Publishing, Inc.
P.O. Box 908
Eureka, Montana 59917
www.lighthousetrails.com

Library of Congress Cataloging-in-Publication Data
Names: Kirkland, Bob (Pastor), author.
Title: Calvinism : none dare call it heresy : spotlight on the life and teachings of John Calvin / Bob Kirkland D.D.
Description: 2nd Edition. | Eureka : Lighthouse Trails Publishing, 2018. |
   Includes bibliographical references.
Identifiers: LCCN 2018007783 | ISBN 9781942423294 (softbound : alk. paper)
Subjects: LCSH: Calvin, Jean, 1509-1564. | Calvinism--Controversial
   literature.
Classification: LCC BX9424.3 .K57 2018 | DDC 230/.42--dc23
LC record available at https://lccn.loc.gov/2018007783

Printed in the United States of America

CONTENTS

Introduction 9

1/Where Calvin Got His Theology 13

2/John Calvin's Manner of Life 17

3/Changing the Meaning of Words to Promote a Theory 25

    What Is T.U.L.I.P.? (A chart) 34

4/Using a Foolish Analogy to Support Calvinism 35

5/Created to Choose and to Reason 43

6/Distorting Scripture To Teach Heresy 57

7/Calvinism's Perseverance 73

8/No Assurance of Salvation 79

9/Think It Through! 85

10/In Conclusion 89

Appendix I: Should Christians Expose Error? 91

Appendix II: A Biblical Perspective on Salvation 95

Appendix III: A Biblical Perspective on Contending for the Faith ...103

Endnotes 111

Scripture Index 119

And it shall come to pass, that
whosoever shall call on the name
of the Lord shall be saved.

(Acts 2:21)

INTRODUCTION

TO CALL SOMETHING HERESY IS CLEARLY A strong accusation and should never be done flippantly. For something to *be* heresy, it must deviate from the fundamental teachings of the Bible. And nothing can be more serious than a deviation from the Gospel itself. Calvinism, as I will show in this book, does present "another gospel."

Scripture takes heresy seriously. According to *Strong's Concordance* and *Thayer's Lexicon*, *heresy* means a "chosen course of thought or action," "an opinion varying from the true exposition of the Christian faith," and "a body of men separating themselves from others and following their own tenets."[1] Many Scriptures command us not to allow heresies or false doctrines to be promoted in the church. While Scripture clearly tells us this, it is often overlooked or even embraced for the sake of "unity."

In Titus 3:10, Paul says, "A man that is an heretick after the first and second admonition reject." Notice the word "admonition." This is a word used when dealing with believers. Romans 15:14 refers to the Christian when it says, "admonish one another." Second Thessalonians 3:14-15 says, "And if any man obey not our word by this epistle, note that man, and have no company with him, that he may be ashamed. Yet count him not as an enemy, but admonish him as a brother."

Today, many churches, ministries, and seminaries are promoting Calvinism. The purpose of this book is to show that the teaching of John Calvin (i.e., Calvinism) is indeed heresy by the Bible's definition of the term. An immediate reaction by some will be to think I am suggesting that all Calvinists are going to Hell. While this is untrue, I will demonstrate that the Calvinist path to salvation becomes more difficult, if not impossible, to those who learn and follow its teachings. Consequently, many drop out and look to another path. Of course, there are many people who call themselves Calvinists who have little idea of what Calvinism actually teaches, or of its history.

While Calvinist scholars claim that Calvinism is complex (and they have indeed created a complex system), the rudiments of it are very basic, and it can be readily understood. I have spent considerable time studying Calvinism over the past forty years with many additional concentrated hours prior to writing this book. So, in spite of its complexities, it is this ready understanding I am presenting in *Calvinism: None Dare Call It Heresy*.

When developing any theological platform, it is essential to have a strong biblical foundation. In the case of Calvinism, it is built on the foundation of erroneous deductions on meanings of words. Of all the Calvinistic materials I have read, I have found continual contradictions by the writers, with the meaning of words of the Bible being changed and redefined in order to make Calvinism work.

John Calvin taught that God will be glorified by bringing billions of people into this world for no other purpose than having them burn in Hell for eternity. This alone depicts a view of God found nowhere in Scripture, and in essence misrepresents God but also creates a platform upon which "another gospel" has been built that is both fatalistic and makes the sacrifice of Christ no longer freely available to *whosoever* may come. Salvation is no longer a matter of choice. Furthermore, the Calvinist can never actually know if he or she is one of "the elect" thereby placing the Calvinist "Gospel" on a foundation of doubt rather than true biblical belief in the substitutionary sacrifice of Christ at Calvary. If that is not heresy, then what is?

By predestination we mean the eternal decree of God, by which he determined with himself whatever he wished to happen with regard to every man. All are not created on equal terms, but some are preordained to eternal life, others to eternal damnation; and, accordingly, as each has been created for one or other of these ends, we say that he has been predestinated to life or to death.[2]—**John Calvin**

1

WHERE CALVIN GOT HIS THEOLOGY

WHEN ONE PREACHER FIRST MEETS another preacher, it usually isn't long until the question will come up concerning where they each received their Bible training. The answer will reveal a lot of information concerning the theology and the philosophy of ministry of the new acquaintance.

Concerning John Calvin's spiritual education, Calvin said:

> Augustine is so much at one with me that, if I wished to write a confession of my faith, it would abundantly satisfy me to quote wholesale from his writings.[1]

WHO WAS AUGUSTINE, AND WHAT DID HE BELIEVE?

Augustine (354-430) has sometimes been referred to as, "the father of the Inquisition" because he set the precedent that force and suppression must be used to stop and control those who were deemed heretics:

> The emperor, he [Augustine] argued, had the duty of suppressing schism and heresy, and indeed of putting pressure on heretics to oblige them to convert. "Compel them to come in" (Luke 14: 23) was given a new and unsuspected meaning. Augustine had become the father of the Inquisition.[2]

In referring to those he considered heretics, Augustine said:

> Why . . . should not the Church use force in compelling her lost sons to return, if the lost sons compelled others to their destruction?"[3]

Augustine also held to many beliefs that line up more with Catholicism than with biblical Christianity. With regard to infant baptism, Augustine stated:

> So that infants, unless they pass into the number of believers through the sacrament [baptism] which was divinely instituted for this purpose, will undoubtedly remain in this darkness.[4]

Let there be then no eternal salvation promised to infants out of our own opinion, without Christ's baptism.[5]

. . . unless this benefit [baptism] has been bestowed upon them [infants], they are manifestly in danger of damnation.[6]

[U]nbaptized infants not only cannot enter into the kingdom of God, but cannot have everlasting life.[7]

Augustine also said things to suggest he believed Mary was sinless as can be seen in his book *On Nature and Grace* in chapter 42 titled "The Blessed Virgin Mary May Have Lived Without Sin."[8] In addition, he believed in purgatory.[9] Regarding salvation, Augustine said:

I should not believe the gospel except as moved by the authority of the Catholic Church.[10]

He made this statement because he believed the only true church was the Roman Catholic Church. He stated:

The Catholic Church alone is the body of Christ. . . . Outside this body, the Holy Spirit giveth life to no one.[11]

This is the man of whom John Calvin based his understanding of the Bible. According to Augustine, anyone outside the Catholic church is going to Hell. Did Calvin not realize that would have to include him?

A YOUNG CONVERT FRESH
OUT OF CATHOLICISM

Within only two years after Calvin declared himself a Protestant, he published his famous *Institutes of the Christian Religion*. In all of Calvin's writing, one will not find a clear testimony of his salvation experience. A statement of his "conversion" can only be found in his book *Commentary on the Psalms* where he writes:

> God by a sudden conversion [referring to his sudden move away from the Catholic Church at the age of 23] subdued and brought my mind to a teachable frame, which was more hardened in such matters than might have been expected from one at my early period of life. Having thus received some taste and knowledge of true godliness I was immediately inflamed with so intense a desire to make progress therein, that although I did not altogether leave off other studies, I yet pursued them with less ardor.[12]

If we assume his vague intellectual testimony of salvation was a genuine salvation experience, he had been a Christian for just about two years when he wrote his *Institutes*, which is a foundational resource for today's Calvinism.

It is interesting to note that during that same two-year period, this man that is held in such high esteem by so many Christians today kept himself on the payroll of the Catholic Church for at least a year.[13]

2

JOHN CALVIN'S MANNER OF LIFE

BERNARD COTTRET, A UNIVERSITY PROFESSOR in France, wrote a book titled, *Calvin: A Biography* in which he clearly shows his admiration for Calvin on several levels. Thus, given that Cottret is not what you would call a critic of Calvin, it lends credibility to the *more* than 36* executions with which Calvin was directly or indirectly involved that are recorded in the book. Cottret documents the dates of executions and the methods of persecution, torture, and execution. He describes the period of time when Calvin had much authority in Geneva; and when Calvin denounced someone as a heretic (often the denouncement came for criticizing or even just questioning Calvin's teachings) that

---

* Some resources regarding the Calvin-related executions have given numbers as high as 58.

person was hunted down. Cottret describes the atmosphere during this time:

> Fear of sorcery and of heretics entailed their retinue of hasty, indeed barbarous remedies: imprisonment, torture, the stake.[1]

Men and women alike endured the torturous imprisonments and deaths.

THREE EXAMPLES OF CALVIN'S PERSECUTIONS

Jacques Gruet, a known opponent of Calvin, was arrested and tortured twice a day for a month in an effort to get him to confess to the accusations against him. Then, on July 26, 1547, he was tied to a stake, his feet were nailed to it, and he was beheaded.[2]

Gruet's book was later found and burned along with his house while his wife was thrown out into the street to watch. This was not unusual behavior to those who dared to challenge or disagree with Calvin:

> Gruet was put to the torture many times (444) during many days . . . In reality such unmeasured use of torture was in Geneva a Calvinistic innovation. Gruet, refusing under the worst stress of torture to incriminate anyone else, at length, in order to end it, pleaded guilty to the charges against him, praying in his last extremity for a speedy death. On July 26, 1547, his half-dead body was beheaded on the scaffold, the torso being tied and the feet nailed thereto. Such were

the judicial methods and mercies of a reformed Christianity, guided by a chief reformer.[3]

Michael Servetus, a scientist, a physician, and theologian was born in Villanova in 1511. He angered Calvin by returning a copy of Calvin's writings with critical comments in the margins. Calvin drew up a doctrine of over thirty official charges against Servetus, one of which was the rejection of John Calvin's teaching concerning infant baptism leading to salvation. Five days into the trial, Calvin wrote, "I hope the death sentence will at least be passed upon him."[4] He also stated regarding Servetus, "If he come, and my influence can avail, I shall not suffer him to depart alive."[5]

Calvin got his wish on October 27, 1553. Servetus was burned at the stake. He was screaming as he was literally baked alive from the feet upward and suffered the heat of the flames for thirty minutes before finally succumbing to one of the most painful and brutal methods of death possible.

Servetus had written a theology book, a copy of which was strapped to the chest of Servetus. The flames from the burning book rose against his face as he screamed in agony.[6]

While Michael Servetus definitely had some unbiblical teachings, such as his rejection of the Trinity, he was, as the late apologist Dave Hunt puts it, "right about some things: that God does not predestine souls to hell and that God is love."[7]

Some have tried to say that Calvin was not responsible for the cruel manner in which Servetus was executed and that all he wanted was for Servetus to be beheaded (obviously, a less painful way to be executed). Brenda Nickel, a former Calvinist who was featured in a documentary film about Reformed Theology, provides some insight:

> Calvin had a long-standing vendetta against Servetus. Servetus foolishly taunted Calvin through letters; thus, Calvin insisted on having him arrested and charged when he entered Geneva. Calvin wanted the death penalty for him. Servetus pleaded with Calvin to be beheaded instead of being burned at the stake, and Calvin was willing to go along with the idea. If Servetus was beheaded instead of burned, then Calvin couldn't be blamed. Beheading, in this case, was attractive to both Servetus and Calvin. Beheading would be seen as a civil crime and free Calvin from having blood on his hands. French reformer William Farel rebuked Calvin for the thought. Since the charge was religious and not civil in nature, Servetus was burned at the stake.
>
> Melanchthon (Luther's friend and successor) praised Calvin for Servetus' death. This execution basically skyrocketed Calvin to fame throughout Europe. It put him on the map, so to speak, as a noteworthy and respected reformer.[8]

Apparently, Calvin must have felt a need to appease himself of guilt in the murders he had helped to institutionalize.

Bernard Cottret also wrote of the persecution of the Anabaptist Belot :

> While he shared the prejudices of his contemporaries against sorcerers, Calvin the churchman remained devoted to one of the church's principal missions, the denunciation of heresy and the condemnation of heretics. For Calvin the greatest heretics were the Anabaptists. They were the internal enemy, as against the papists, who threatened the development of the "true faith" from outside. Papists, moreover, were not heretics in the strict sense; their errors were predictable, almost programmed, and less dangerous on the whole than those original thoughts that risked affecting the Reformed world itself. In 1545 the Anabaptist Belot held that the Old Testament was abolished by the New. This point of view might be debatable theologically, but did it justify the torture inflicted on poor Belot after he was chained and his invectives against Calvin were laughed at?[9]

Gruet, Servetus, and Belot were not the only ones to be persecuted for speaking against John Calvin and his institutes:

> With dictatorial control over the populace ("he ruled as few sovereigns have done"), Calvin imposed his brand of Christianity upon the citizenry with floggings, imprisonments, banishments, and burnings at the stake. Calvin has been called

"the Protestant Pope" and "the Genevese dictator" who "would tolerate in Geneva the opinions of only one person, his own."[10]

It puzzles me immensely why anyone would think that God would use such a man as Calvin to be a great leader of Christianity?

In 1 Corinthians 11:1, Paul said, "Be ye followers (imitators) of me, even as I also am of Christ." Was John Calvin an imitator of Christ in his actions? I see no answer to that question but a resounding, "Not at all!"

CHRIST OUR EXAMPLE

Jesus said in Matthew 5:44, "But I say unto you, Love your enemies, bless them that curse you, do good to them that hate you, and pray for them which despitefully use you, and persecute you."

Jesus was persecuted for over thirty years and finally crucified. In Luke 23:34, we read how Jesus responded to His enemies. He said, "Father, forgive them; for they know not what they do." And in John 13:15, Jesus said, "I have given you an example, that ye should do as I have done to you."

Dave Hunt, who wrote the Calvinist expose, *What Love is This?*, said:

Perhaps Calvin thought he was God's instrument to force Irresistible Grace (a key doctrine in Calvinism) upon the citizens of Geneva, Switzerland— even upon those who proved their unworthiness by resisting to the death. He unquestionably did his best to be irresistible in imposing "righteousness," but what he imposed and the manner in which he imposed it was far from grace and the teachings and example of Christ.[11]

EXAMPLES OF THE FOLLOWERS OF CHRIST

Stephen's persecutors did not write a note on the margin of his sermon outline; they were smashing his head in with rocks. He cried loudly, "Lord, lay not this sin to their charge" (Acts 7:60). When Peter, James, John, and Paul were persecuted, they had no desire to strike back at their persecutors. They responded the way they did because they were all under the control of the Holy Spirit. "[T]he fruit of the Spirit is love" (Galatians 5:22). But Calvin had no real persecutors and responded to those who opposed him by having them imprisoned, brutally tortured, and murdered.

Bible Christians who are born again and indwelt by the Holy Spirit never hope the death sentence is passed upon their persecutors as did Calvin when people disagreed with him.

WHAT SPIRIT CONTROLLED JOHN CALVIN?

The primary teaching in Calvinism is the teaching on "election" in that the majority of people God created, He did not elect to save nor did He love them. In fact, He hated them from before they were even born. Under the Calvinist view of election, wherein God does not love every human being or desires that each one come to faith and be saved, it makes sense that John Calvin did not have God's love toward those he saw as his unsaved fellow man. After all, if *God* does not even love them, why should he? It is this reasoning that would have made it easy for Calvin to justify the torture and murder of people whom he believed, in his own estimation, to be heretics.

But the Bible says that God is love. And He is righteous, true, faithful, and just. Such are fruits of the Spirit as described in Galatians 5:22, and love is the first one mentioned.

It is hard not to believe that John Calvin was under the influence of some other spirit than the Holy Spirit. You will have to look long and hard to find anything in Calvin's writings about love. It is certainly not obvious in his manner of life.

3

CHANGING THE MEANING OF WORDS TO PROMOTE A THEORY

THE ONLY WAY CALVINISTS CAN SUPPORT their theory from the Bible is to alter the meaning of Bible words or take them out of context. When a Calvinist teaches "whosoever will," he means whosoever "God wills." Calvinist Arthur (A. W.) Pink (1886-1952), who "sparked a renewed interest in the exposition of Calvinism,"[1] wrote, "The fact is, the love of God is a truth for the saints only."[2] He said:

> [T]he "world" in John 3:16 must, in the final
> analysis, refer to the world of God's people.[3]

When a Calvinist talks about the "sovereignty" of God, he has his own definition of the word *sovereignty* (as he does with the word *depravity*). *Easton's Illustrated Bible Dictionary* says that the sovereignty of God is "[H]is absolute right to do all things according to his own good pleasure."[4]

God, in His sovereignty, in His absolute right to do all things according to His own good pleasure, has established some laws for mankind. For example, the Bible says, "except ye repent ye shall all likewise perish" (Luke 13:3). God, in His sovereignty, has determined that the sinner who does not repent will not gain eternal life.

Considering that the word "sovereignty" is not in the Bible and considering the actual meaning of the word, rather than Calvin's distorted meaning (which he needed to support his theory), we see God is no less sovereign because He, according to His own good pleasure, gives man a free will making him capable of repenting of his sin and receiving Christ as his Savior.

Again, when A. W. Pink said the "'world' in John 3:16 must, in the final analysis, refer to the world of God's people," he continued, saying, "Must we say, for there is no alternative solution."[5] The dictionary says, a solution is, "an answer to a problem." John 3:16 presents no problem unless you are a Calvinist needing a "solution" to support your theory. The way a Calvinist solves his problem is to simply change the meaning of words in the Bible and in the dictionary to mean what they need to mean to support their position.

Calvinist writers have made many declarations that God has decreed everything that would happen in this world, from Adam's sin to the doom of billions of people in Hell. The only way they can maintain their theory is to change the words "world" and "whosoever" to "elect."

Since Calvinists can change these words in John 3:16, it must be all right to change these words in John 15:18-19.

USING THE CALVINISTIC "SOLUTION" IN JOHN 15:18-19

John 15:18-19 says:

> If the world hate you, ye know that it hated me before it hated you. If ye were of the world, the world would love his own: but because ye are not of the world, but I have chosen you out of the world, therefore the world hateth you.

Using the Calvinist "solution" of changing the word "world" as they did in John 3:16 so that it means elect, John 15:18-19 now must read:

> If the elect hate you, who are the elect, ye know that the elect hated me before the elect hated you who are elect. If ye elect were of the elect, the elect would love his own elect: but because ye elect are not of the elect, but I have chosen you elect out of the elect, therefore the elect hateth you elect who are elect.

No doubt, this is a foolish translation of the verse; however, it is no more foolish than the Calvinistic interpretation of John 3:16.

The word "world" is found over 240 times in the Bible. A few times, the Greek word obviously reveals different meanings; however, the word "world" never means Calvin's

27

so-called elect. Never! The only reason for rejecting the obvious simple-to-understand meaning of the words "whosoever" or "world" in John 3:16 is to support Calvin's heresy.

ALL MEANS ALL

Joshua 6:3 says, ". . . *all* ye men of war."

Psalm 31:23 says, ". . . *all* ye his saints."

Psalm 31:24 says, ". . . *all* ye that hope in the LORD."

Psalm 32:11 says, ". . . *all* ye that are upright in heart."

Psalm 134:1 says, ". . . *all* ye servants of the LORD."

Luke 13:27 says, ". . . *all* ye workers of iniquity."

Romans 5:12 says, ". . . *all* have sinned."

Galatians 3:8 says, ". . . *all* nations be blessed."

Revelation 19:5 says, ". . . *all* ye his servants, and ye that fear him." (emphasis added in the above verses)

Nobody argues that "all" means "all" in Romans 5:12 when it says, ". . . all have sinned." The only reason to suggest "all" means something else in Acts 17:30, when God commands "all men every where to repent," is because Calvinists need to change this to provide a "solution" to support their view.

Listen to the doubletalk of A. W. Pink when he says:

> That God commandeth "all men" to repent is but the enforcing of His righteous claims as the moral Governor of the world.[6]

What Pink is saying here is that God is not sincere when he says "all men every where to repent," but only saying it to show how righteous and moral He is.

Then Pink uses Acts 5:31 to say:

> [T]his Scripture does not declare that it is God's pleasure to "give repentance" (Acts 5:31) to all men everywhere.[7]

Let's see what Acts 5:31 actually says:

> Him hath God exalted with his right hand to be a Prince and a Saviour, for to give repentance to Israel, and forgiveness of sins.

In this passage of Scripture, Peter and the apostles declared to the High Priest and Council that God had made Jesus a Prince and Savior bringing repentance and forgiveness of sins to Israel. Their audience was Jewish, and therefore, their speech pertained to the Jews they were addressing; however, they were not saying that the Jews were the only ones to be saved and forgiven.

But Pink uses this verse to support his theory that it is *not* God's pleasure to "give repentance" to all men everywhere. In taking Acts 5:31 completely out of context, perhaps Pink did not realize that by trying to use this verse to fit his own theology, he was actually saying that only Jewish people will ever get saved. Hence, all Gentiles will end up in Hell. That would include Pink himself. And because there is ultimately no free will in Calvinism, there is nothing anyone can do about it.

MORE VERSES USING CALVINISM'S "SOLUTION" OF CHANGING OF WORDS

First John 2:2 says, "And he is the propitiation for our sins: and not for ours only, but also for the sins *of the whole world*" (emphasis added).

"Calvinist Solution"—And he is the propitiation for the sins of the elect: and not for the elect only, but also for the sins of the elect.

Ezra 8:22 says, "The hand of our God is upon all them for good that seek him; but his power and his wrath is against all them that forsake him."

"Calvinist Solution"—The hand of our God is upon all the elect for good that seek him; even though they have no free will to seek him, but his power and his wrath is against all the non-elect that forsake him, even though they are dead and have no free will to forsake him.

Psalm 10:4 says, "The wicked, through the pride of his countenance, will not seek after God." Psalm 11:6 says, "Upon the wicked he shall rain snares, fire and brimstone."

"Calvinist Solution"—The wicked, who are not among God's elect, through the pride of his countenance, pride that God put in his heart, cannot seek after God; however, even though God has withheld from the wicked non-elect the ability to seek after God, He shall rain snares, fire and brimstone.

Psalm 13:5 says, "But I have trusted in thy mercy; my heart shall rejoice in thy salvation."

"Calvinist Solution"—But I can't trust in thy mercy because I am dead and therefore not capable of trusting; my heart can't rejoice in thy salvation because I can't trust in thy mercy and besides I do not have any assurance that you included me in your mercy.

CALVINISTS TEACH ALL MEN ARE TOTALLY DEPRAVED

It is true that all people have depraved and sinful natures, and no person merits salvation. However, the word "total" means, "entirely, to the full." The word "depraved" means "morally corrupt." To suggest that all people in the world are "totally immoral" is ridiculous. None of the neighbors on the street where I live confess to be saved, but that does not make them *totally* immoral. We must not forget that God has put a conscience in people so that we know or have a sense of right and wrong. Even an unsaved person can feel

31

remorse and regret when he has done something wrong. If he was totally depraved, he would not have the capability to do that (see Romans 1: 19-20).

The Bible speaks again and again of some people who are more corrupt than others. Ezekiel 16:47 says, "[T]hou wast corrupted more than they in all thy ways." Judges 2:19 says that they "corrupted themselves more than their fathers." First Kings 16:25 says, "Omri . . . did worse than all that were before him." Jeremiah 7:26 says, "[T]hey did worse than their fathers."

However, we must remember that Calvinists have their own special meaning for words. To a Calvinist total depravity means "total inability." The common dictionary meaning of inability is, *not having the quality or state of being able to do something.* Calvinism says that because all mankind is dead in trespasses and sins" (Ephesians 2:1-4), they cannot respond in any way to receive Christ as their Savior.

QUOTES FROM WELL-KNOWN CALVINISTS

A [spiritually] dead man . . . cannot exercise faith in Jesus Christ.[8]—Gordon H. Clark

The sinner . . . is utterly incapable of willing anything.[9]—A. W. Pink

A corpse does not cry out for help.[10]—Arthur Custance

[W]e have no more to do with our spiritual birth than we had with our natural birth.[11]—A.W. Pink

[E]ven if what he or she does is simply to repent and believe the gospel, God's grace is seriously, albeit unwittingly, compromised.[12]—Sam Storms

[T]he sinner is of himself neither capable nor willing to receive that salvation.[13]—Herman Hoeksema

The Bible stresses the total inability of fallen man to respond positively to the law of God.[14]—Kenneth Talbot and Gary Crampton

[T]he sinner, of himself, cannot repent and believe.[15]—A.W. Pink

WHAT IS T.U.L.I.P.?

T stands for "Total Depravity." Man is completely and wholly depraved and has no ability whatsoever to respond (repent or believe) to God until he is first "regenerated" by God.

U stands for "Unconditional Election." God determined before the foundation of the world whom He would save and whom He would send to Hell. Man would have no choice or free will to either accept or reject Christ as Savior.

L stands for "Limited Atonement." Christ's atonement on the Cross was not for everyone but rather just for the "elect."

I stands for "Irresistible Grace." Faith is something "God irresistibly bestowed upon the elect without their having believed anything . . . By such reasoning, man . . . can't even hear the gospel—much less respond to the pleadings of Christ."[1]

P stands for "Perseverance of the Saints." This is what Calvinists say gives them the assurance of eternal security, but in actuality "the emphasis is upon the *believer's* faithfulness in persevering—not upon God's keeping power. . . . uncertainty as to one's ultimate salvation is, in fact, built into the very fabric of Calvinism itself."[2]

4

USING A FOOLISH ANALOGY TO SUPPORT CALVINISM

EPHESIANS 2:1 SAYS, "AND YOU HATH HE quickened, who were dead in trespasses and sins." Calvinists say, "Since he is dead, it is impossible for him to believe." This is a foolish analogy! The Bible is referring here to spiritual death not physical death. In Genesis 2:17, God warned Adam and Eve not to eat of the forbidden fruit. He said, "[F]or in the day that thou eatest thereof thou shalt surely die." They ate, but they did not die physically that same day. They died spiritually. A person who is physically dead cannot receive Christ as his Savior, but neither can he speak, breathe, laugh, walk, live a righteous life, or sin.

THE PHILIPPIAN JAILER

Acts 16:30 says the unsaved Philippian jailer asked Paul, "[W]hat must I do to be saved?"

Paul did not say, "You can do nothing to be saved, you are dead." He said, "Believe on the Lord Jesus Christ, and thou shalt be saved" (v. 31).

Isaiah 1:18 says:

> Come now, and *let us reason together,* saith the LORD: though your sins be as scarlet, they shall be as white as snow; though they be red like crimson, they shall be as wool. (emphasis added)

This is not written to physically dead people. A physically dead man cannot reason anything. It is written to spiritually dead, unsaved people concerning salvation. If a spiritually dead man is never capable of reasoning spiritual things, why would God command him to do so?

THE BIBLE GIVES MANY EXAMPLES OF SPIRITUALLY DEAD PEOPLE EXERCISING FAITH

A Roman Centurion Exercised Faith (Matthew 8:10, 13):

> Verily I say unto you, I have not found so great faith, no, not in Israel. . . . Jesus said unto the centurion, Go thy way; and as thou hast believed, so be it done unto thee. And his servant was healed in the selfsame hour.

A Father of A Demon Possessed Child Exercised Faith (Mark 9:23-24):

Jesus said . . . all things are possible to him that believeth. . . . And straightway the father of the child cried out, and said with tears, Lord, I believe. [Jesus cast the demon out of the boy.]

A Woman With A Disease Exercised Faith (Matthew 9:21-22):

[S]he said . . . If I may but touch his garment, I shall be whole. Jesus . . . said, Daughter, be of good comfort; thy faith hath made thee whole.

Two Blind Men Exercised Faith (Matthew 9:28-30):

Jesus saith unto them, Believe ye that I am able to do this? They said unto him, Yea, Lord. Then touched he their eyes, saying, According to your faith be it unto you. And their eyes were opened.

The Canaanite Mother Exercised Faith (Matthew 15:28):

Jesus . . . said unto her, O woman, great is thy faith: be it unto thee even as thou wilt. And her daughter was made whole from that very hour.

A Blind Man Exercised Faith (Luke 18:42-43):

Jesus said unto him, Receive thy sight: thy faith hath saved thee. And immediately he received his sight.

A Man Named Jairus Exercised Faith (Luke 8:50, 55):

[Jesus] answered [Jairus], saying, Fear not: believe only, and she shall be made whole. . . . her spirit came again, and she arose straightway.

A Man Kicked Out of The Temple Exercised Faith (John 9:35-38):

Jesus heard that they had cast him out; and when he had found him, he said unto him, Dost thou believe on the Son of God? He answered and said, Who is he, Lord, that I might believe on him? And Jesus said unto him, Thou hast both seen him, and it is he that talketh with thee. And he said, Lord, I believe. And he worshipped him.

CALVINISTS REVERSE GOD'S METHOD OF SALVATION

The Calvinist says a person must be born again before he can repent or believe. In John 20:31, Jesus says quite the opposite to that:

But these are written, that ye might believe that Jesus is the Christ, the Son of God; and that believing ye might have life through his name.

It is clear the Bible teaches that man will not seek God on his own and that he needs the indwelling of the Holy Spirit to live out the repentant lifestyle, but there is not a single verse in the Bible to indicate man is incapable of responding to the conviction of the Holy Spirit to repent of his sin and receive Christ as his personal Savior.

In John 6:44, Jesus said, "No man can come to me, except the Father which hath sent me draw him"; however, unsaved people can exercise their will to disobey. Jesus said, in John 4:48, "ye will not believe." He did not say ye *cannot* believe!

Jesus said in John 5:40, "Ye will not come to me, that ye might have life." Notice that Jesus indicated they must come first to have life. The Calvinist, to be consistent with his belief of man's inability to respond to the Gospel, will have to turn this verse around to say, "And ye will not have life that ye may come to me." But this does not work either because either way, man is exercising his will, which is something Calvinists teach he is incapable of doing.

In Matthew 23:37, Jesus said:

> O Jerusalem, Jerusalem . . . how often would I have gathered thy children together, even as a hen gathereth her chickens under her wings, and ye would not!

Some Calvinists use John 6:44 in an effort to prove total inability. Here the Bible says, "No man can come to me, except the Father which hath sent me draw him." However, John 12:32 says, "And I, if I be lifted up from the earth, will draw all men unto me." Then in Revelation 22:17, the last invitation in the Bible, says:

> And the Spirit and the bride say, Come. And let him that heareth say, Come. And let him that is athirst come. And whosoever will, let him take the water of life freely.

We see then that while it is the Holy Spirit's work to draw men to the Savior, it is incumbent on each individual to respond of his own free will prior to conversion.

Acts 17:30 says God "commandeth all men everywhere to repent." Romans 14:11-12 says:

> For it is written, As I live, saith the Lord, every knee shall bow to me, and every tongue shall confess to God. So then every one of us shall give account of himself to God.

Every person in this world has a God-given responsibility to repent and be saved, and one day every person will be held accountable. Jesus said in Luke 13:3, "Except ye repent, ye shall all likewise perish." There is not a group of non-elect who will be able to say, "Lord, I did not repent and trust Christ as Savior because I was totally depraved and unable to believe."

Besides, if we translate the verse using the Calvinistic "solution," it would read, "Except ye repent, ye shall all likewise perish except ye all won't perish because some of you are elect and are saved by God's irresistible grace."

Second Peter 3:9 says the Lord is "not willing that any should perish, but that all should come to repentance." God holds us responsible for our life on Earth, and we are commanded to repent of our sin and trust Christ as our Savior.

Calvinists teach that man cannot repent or believe the Gospel until he is born again. They teach that this new birth is brought about by God who chooses certain elect individuals and regenerates them making them capable of believing. They say man does not have a free will by which he is able to come to Christ for salvation.

Acts 11:18 says plainly that, "God also to the Gentiles granted repentance unto life." Repentance comes first and the result of repentance is life. Remember, John 5:40 says, "Ye will not come to me, that ye might have life." The coming is first, the life is second.

Will you believe the godly men who wrote under the inspiration of the Holy Spirit, or will you believe a man who wrote under the inspiration of the Catholic Bishop Augustine and who was filled with hatred for those who disagreed with him? Remember, Calvin said, "Augustine is so much at one with me that, if I wished to write a confession of my faith, it would abundantly satisfy me to quote wholesale from his writings."[1]

THE BIBLE ALWAYS PUTS "BELIEVING" FIRST

Whosoever believeth in him should not perish, but have eternal life. (John 3:15)

Whosoever believeth in him should not perish, but have everlasting life. (John 3:16)

He that believeth on the Son hath everlasting life. (John 3:36)

He that heareth my word, and believeth on him that sent me, hath everlasting life [and] is passed from death unto life. (John 5:24)

[E]very one which . . . believeth on him, may have everlasting life. (John 6:40)

The Bible also says:

But these are written, that ye might believe that Jesus is the Christ, the Son of God; and that believing ye might have life through his name. (John 20:31)

5

CREATED TO CHOOSE AND TO REASON

BACK TO THE BEGINNING

GENESIS 1:26 SAYS, "AND GOD SAID, LET US make man in our image, after our likeness." To be made in the image and likeness of God is multifaceted. Scripture, of course, makes it clear that man is not divine or a part of God, and it would be wrong for us to think so. However, it would also be wrong to minimize man to something he is not by stripping him of the abilities and attributes God has given him. So, even though Adam fell, man still has a soul. And man still has the ability to choose and to reason. These attributes were not taken from man when Adam fell as is very evident by simple observation. In Scripture, God commands the sinner to reason, to choose, and to repent. God's grace operates in our lives in a viable active way (not a passive way).

But with Calvinism, grace is actually minimized, and God is made small by saying that the only way God can be sovereign is by allowing no free will at all (i.e., no choices, no reasoning). The Calvinist view has God operating in a way that is contrary to His original and unchanging design.

GOD GAVE ADAM A COMMAND

Genesis 2:15-17 says:

> And the LORD God took the man, and put him into the garden of Eden to dress it and to keep it. And the LORD God commanded the man, saying, Of every tree of the garden thou mayest freely eat: But of the tree of the knowledge of good and evil, thou shalt not eat of it: for in the day that thou eatest thereof thou shalt surely die.

As I pointed out earlier, A. W. Pink's book *The Sovereignty of God* says man is "utterly incapable of willing anything."[1] What does the Bible say? It says, "God commanded the man." If man was created without a free will and the ability to cause things to happen, there would be no need for this command or any other command found in the Scriptures.

In Genesis 3:6, we find Satan tempting Eve to disobey God. It says, "She took of the fruit thereof, and did eat, and gave also unto her husband with her; and he did eat."

ADAM AND EVE MADE DECISIONS

Both Adam and Eve made a decision, each of their own free will, to disobey God. To suggest, as the Calvinists do, that God forced them to sin, we would have to change the verse above from "Thou shalt not eat of it" to "I will make you eat of it." This is foolish and makes God the Author of sin. It is not only heresy, it is blasphemy! The Bible frequently describes God's character and nature (e.g., Titus 1:2: God cannot lie), and He is described as a holy, righteous, loving, judging, honest, merciful, perfect God. He is never described as a God of sin; on the contrary, Scripture says, "God cannot be tempted with evil neither tempteth he any man" (James 1:13).

God confronted Adam and asked, "Hast thou eaten of the tree, whereof I commanded thee that thou shouldest not eat?" (Genesis 3:11). Verse 17 of chapter three continues:

> And unto Adam he said, Because thou hast hearkened unto the voice of thy wife, and hast eaten of the tree, of which I commanded thee, saying, Thou shalt not eat of it: cursed is the ground for thy sake; in sorrow shalt thou eat of it all the days of thy life.

Adam chose to listen to Eve rather than obey God. As a result of choosing to sin, the spirit of man died and, therefore, must be "born again." Jesus went into much detail concerning being "born again" in John chapter three. The Bible plainly teaches that when a person is convicted by the Holy Spirit to repent of his or her sin, a decision must be made. If man chooses to trust Christ as Savior, the spirit of man is "born again." We read in Ephesians 2:1, "And you hath he quickened, who were dead in trespasses and sins."

ADAM AND EVE SENT FROM THE GARDEN

God sent Adam and Eve from the garden because they could have used their free will to eat of the tree of life and live in their sinful state forever. Genesis 3, verses 22-24 read:

> [A]nd now, lest he put forth his hand, and take also of the tree of life, and eat, and live for ever: Therefore the LORD God sent him forth from the garden of Eden, to till the ground from whence he was taken. So he drove out the man and he placed at the east of the garden of Eden Cherubims, and a flaming sword which turned every way, to keep the way of the tree of life.

There would have been no need for the Cherubims with the flaming sword if man did not have a free will; it was for the very reason that man had free will that God had to block the way for Adam to get to the tree of life! What kind of game do the Calvinists think God is playing?

CAIN AND ABEL MADE CHOICES

In Genesis 4, we read how Abel decided to follow God and Cain decided to do things his own way. Verse 16 says, "And

Cain went out from the presence of the LORD." Cain also decided to persecute the one who followed God, even to the death. To say God put it in the heart of Cain to go out from the presence of the Lord and then kill his brother is wicked, ridiculous, and attacks the very character of God.

HOW CALVINISTS NEED TO RE-INTERPRET THE CREATION ACCOUNT TO BE CONSISTENT

To support Calvin's wicked-God theory, we would need to change the creation account to read, "In the beginning, God created the heaven and the earth . . . And God said, Let us make people with no free will. And then God said, 'We will trick them into thinking they have a free will by saying . . . of every tree of the garden thou mayest freely eat. But of the tree of the knowledge of good and evil, thou shalt not eat of it: for in the day that thou eatest thereof, thou shalt surely die.' We will let them think they can choose to disobey."

Calvin's distorted account would also need to say, "Because they didn't really have a free will, God ordained it from the beginning for them to eat the fruit thereof. Then God confronted Adam and asked, Hast thou eaten of the tree, whereof I commanded thee that thou shouldest not eat? . . . Cursed is the ground for thy sake; in sorrow shalt thou eat of it all the days of thy life." Concerning Cain and Abel, the story would need to be changed to read, "God then forced Cain to kill his brother and then put a curse upon him for doing it."

It should be noted here that Calvinists (as did John Calvin) confuse God's foreknowledge with predestination (or even just disregard foreknowledge altogether). God *knew* that Judas would betray Jesus for thirty pieces of silver ahead of time according to Zechariah 11:12-13, but God had no hand in *making* these things happen. God also *knew* that the Jewish people would be scattered throughout the world; and even though they would prosper wherever they went, they would also be hated and persecuted among the nations. But God never sanctioned the persecution and attempted annihilation of the Jews under Hitler's regime. Instead, we read in Scripture "And I will bless them that bless thee, and curse him that curseth thee: and in thee shall all families of the earth be blessed" (Genesis 12:3) and "he that toucheth you toucheth the apple of his eye" (Zechariah 2:8). The persecutors of the Jews, as in the case of Adolph Hitler, were therefore held fully responsible for what they did.

But the Calvinist is locked into a fatalistic view where God preordains everything and therefore approves of everything. Hence, Scripture, like the above verses, must be twisted and distorted to accommodate a malicious "God."

GOD COMMANDS PEOPLE TO TRUST HIM— PSALM 4:5: "PUT YOUR TRUST IN THE LORD."

Trust in the LORD. (Psalm 37:3)

GOD FORCES NOBODY TO TRUST HIM

. . . trusted not in his salvation. (Psalm 78:22)

. . . trusted in thy wickedness. (Isaiah 47:10)

. . . trusted in falsehood. (Jeremiah 13:25)

. . . trusted in thy works. (Jeremiah 48:7)

. . . trusted in her treasures. (Jeremiah 49:4)

MAN IS COMMANDED TO SUBMIT

. . . submit yourselves. (1 Corinthians 16:16)

. . . submit yourselves. (Ephesians 5:22)

. . . submit yourselves. (Colossians 3:18)

. . . submit yourselves. (Hebrews 13:17)

. . . submit yourselves. (James 4:7)

. . . submit yourselves. (1 Peter 2:13)

. . . submit yourselves. (1 Peter 5:5)

GOD NEVER FORCES ANYONE TO SUBMIT

. . . they hearkened not. (Exodus 6:9)

. . . they hearkened not. (Exodus 16:20)

. . . they hearkened not. (1 Samuel 2:25)

. . . they hearkened not. (2 Kings 21:9)

. . . they hearkened not. (Jeremiah 7:24)

. . . they hearkened not. (Jeremiah 7:26)

. . . they hearkened not. (Jeremiah 36:31)

MAN IS COMMANDED TO "REASON" ABOUT SALVATION

Isaiah 1:18 says:

> Come now, and let us reason together, saith the
> LORD: though your sins be as scarlet, they shall
> be as white as snow; though they be red like crim-
> son, they shall be as wool.

Matthew 16:7 says, ". . . they reasoned."

Matthew 21:25 says, ". . . they reasoned."

Mark 2:8 says, ". . . they reasoned."

Mark 8:16 says, ". . . they reasoned."

Mark 11:31 says, ". . . they reasoned."

Luke 20:5 says, ". . . they reasoned."

Luke 20:14 says, ". . . they reasoned."

Acts 18:4 says, ". . . he reasoned and persuaded."

Acts 24:25 says, ". . . he reasoned . . . Felix trembled."

Acts 28:29 says, ". . . the Jews departed, and had great reasoning among themselves."

AFTER REASONING, MAN HAS A FREE WILL TO COME TO HIS OWN DECISION

We read in Mark 2:6 that the scribes Jesus spoke to were, ". . . reasoning in their hearts." Mark 7:9 tells us after their reasoning, they made a decision. Jesus rebuked them for their decision (but did not force them to change) saying, "[Y]e reject the commandment of God." Hosea 4:6 refers to those who "rejected knowledge." Second Kings 17:15 says, "They rejected his statutes, and his covenant." Contrary to Calvinism, man can reason concerning salvation, and man can reject or receive the salvation God offers him through the Gospel of Jesus Christ.

GOD COMMANDS MAN TO WALK IN HIS WAYS, BUT HE FORCES NO ONE

Isaiah 30:21 says, "This is the way, walk ye in it." Psalm 81:12 states, ". . . they walked in their own counsels."

GOD COMMANDS MAN TO BE HOLY BUT HE FORCES NOBODY

Leviticus 20:7 says "[B]e ye holy: for I am the LORD your God." Deuteronomy 9:12 says, ". . . [they] corrupted themselves."

FREE WILL AND THE TEN COMMANDMENTS

Thou shalt have no other gods before me. (Exodus 20:3)

. . . served other gods. (Deuteronomy 17:3)

Thou shalt not make . . . any graven image. (Exodus 20:4)

. . . moved him to jealousy with their graven images. (Psalm 78:58)

Thou shalt not take the name of the LORD thy God in vain. (Exodus 20:7)

For they . . . take thy name in vain. (Psalm 139:20)

Remember the sabbath day, to keep it holy. (Exodus 20:8)

. . . ye do, and profane the sabbath day? (Nehemiah 13:17)

Honour thy father and thy mother. (Exodus 20:12)

. . . children . . . rise up against their parents. (Matthew 10:21)

Thou shalt not kill. (Exodus 20:13)

They . . . murder the fatherless. (Psalm 94:6)

Thou shalt not commit adultery. (Exodus 20:14)

[T]hey commit adultery. (Jeremiah 23:14)

Thou shalt not steal. (Exodus 20:15)

[S]teal no more. (Ephesians 4:28)

Thou shalt not bear false witness. (Exodus 20:16)

[F]alse witnesses are risen up against me. (Psalm 27:12)

Thou shalt not covet. (Exodus 20:17)

I coveted them, and took them. (Joshua 7:21)

CALVIN'S TEACHING OF UNCONDITIONAL ELECTION

According to Calvinism, if we are to be saved, God chooses (elects) us to salvation. Calvinism teaches, "A man is not saved because he believes in Christ; he believes in Christ because he is saved." In other words,

The elect of God are chosen by Him to be His children, in order that they might be *made* to believe, not because He *foresaw* that they *would* believe.[2] (emphasis added)

MORE HERESY

By his unconditional election theory, Calvin meant that some are elected to Heaven while others are elected to Hell. It is wholly on God's part, and we have nothing to do with our eternal destiny. This means God decided before we were born that we are going to burn in Hell forever or be in Heaven forever. We are simply a pawn in God's big chess game. Calvinism further teaches that God could be glorified by bringing your family into the world for the express purpose of tormenting them in Hell for eternity. *This is wickedness and is not the God of the Bible!*

Lest you think I have misrepresented John Calvin, we will let him speak for himself. In his *Institutes of the Christian Religion,* Volume 3, Calvin stated:

[S]ome are preordained to eternal life, others to eternal damnation; and, accordingly, as each has been created for one or other of these ends, we say that he has been predestinated to life or to death.[3]

This is the view you will find throughout the teachings and sermons of Calvinist preachers and authors. ·

COULD GOD BE GLORIFIED SENDING YOUR MOTHER TO HELL?

According to Calvinism, it might be your mother, your little boy, your daughter, your wife, and all the children in the church nursery whom God will delight in sending to Hell. It might even be you! After all, praying "Lord, be merciful to me, a sinner" is not going to get you to Heaven if God has determined you are going to Hell!

One Calvinist preacher said the following:

> You have made heaven mourn; you have made earth sad; you have dug hell for yourself! Confess your iniquity with shame and with confusion of face! Bow down before the God of mercy and acknowledge that *if He spares you*, it will be His free mercy [i.e., election] that shall do it—but if He destroys you, *you shall not have one word to say* against the justice of the solemn sentence![4] (emphasis added)

In other words, you can cry out to the Lord in humility and repentance and ask Him to save your soul, and He may or may not do it, and there is nothing you can do to gain salvation. Yet, the Bible is filled with verses declaring that God is a merciful God to those who call upon Him. God has ordained to show mercy on those who call upon His name.

WHY ARE PEOPLE EVEN DRAWN TO CALVINISM?

As we are witnessing today, many people are being drawn to Calvinism (including many young people). In our age of uncertainty, Calvinism seems to offer some security in the thought that God has preordained everything. This would presumably put some order into our chaotic world. Unfortunately, once someone has become fully engulfed in Calvinism, it offers no true security. It leaves a person without knowing what direction things will go but with clinging to nothing more than a fatalistic view of life—where things are locked in, and there is nothing anyone can do about it.

Unfortunately, Calvinism is a direct attack on the Gospel. The Gospel is activated by faith (whosoever *believeth*) but the fatalism of Calvinism can say no more than "what will be will be." This is not biblical faith but actually a form of unbelief in that it leaves the recipient in doubt of his future. Although Calvinism seems to offer hope, in reality and in truth, it leaves a person in a lifelong quest of wondering if he is one of the elect. How totally opposite this is to the Gospel the Bible offers where the Good News of Jesus Christ offers hope and belief in it offers certainty:

> Now faith is the substance of things hoped for, the evidence of things not seen. (Hebrews 11:1)

> These things have I written unto you that believe on the name of the Son of God; that ye may know that ye have eternal life, and that ye may believe on the name of the Son of God. (1 John 5:13)

6

DISTORTING SCRIPTURE TO TEACH HERESY

IN AN EFFORT TO SUPPORT THEIR THEORY, Calvinists will quote part of Ephesians 1:4. The first part of the verse says, "[H]e hath chosen us in him before the foundation of the world." However, the entire verse reads:

> According as he hath *chosen* us in him before the foundation of the world, *that* we should be holy and without blame before him in love. (emphasis added)

This verse says nothing about being chosen for Heaven or Hell. It speaks of how God has chosen for Christians to live.

Calvinists also like to quote part of John 15:16, "Ye have not chosen me, but I have chosen you. . . ." The entire verse reads:

> Ye have not chosen me, but I have chosen you, and ordained you, that ye should go and bring forth fruit, and that your fruit should remain: that whatsoever ye shall ask of the Father in my name, he may give it you.

Again, this verse says nothing about being chosen for Heaven or Hell. It says God has chosen that Christians should bear fruit. The fruit of a Christian is other Christians. Proverbs 11:30 says:

> The fruit of the righteous is a tree of life; and he that winneth souls is wise.

In Acts 10:34, the Bible says that "God is no respecter of persons." That means your mother, your little boy, your daughter, your wife, and all the children in the church nursery and you are included when God closed out His Bible with the invitation, ". . . whosoever will, let him take the water of life freely" (Revelation 22:17). The Bible also says in 2 Peter 3:9:

> [God] is . . . not willing that any should perish, but that *all* should come to repentance. (emphasis added)

First Timothy 2:4 refers to God as such:

Who will have all men to be saved, and to come unto the knowledge of the truth.

Calvinist teachers go to great lengths to destroy the plain meaning of this verse. They say "all" doesn't mean "all." There is no end of their interpretations of this verse using their, "This is what the Bible says, but this is what it means" system.

CALVINISM TEACHES SOME PEOPLE ARE PREDESTINED BY GOD TO BURN IN HELL

God has His controlling hand on the affairs of men. He selects individuals like Abraham, Isaac, Jacob, and David as instruments to do certain things. God chose the nation of Israel for a specific purpose. God has chosen people like John the Baptist for a special purpose.

TO TEACH THAT GOD HAS PREDESTINED ANYONE TO BE BORN ONLY TO BURN IN HELL FOR ETERNITY IS HERESY!

Ephesians 1:3-4 says:

Blessed be the God and Father of our Lord Jesus Christ, who hath blessed us with all spiritual blessings in heavenly places in Christ: According as he hath chosen us in him before the foundation of the world, that we should be holy and without blame before him in love.

Romans 8:29-30 says:

> For whom he did foreknow, he also did predestinate to be conformed to the image of his Son, that he might be the firstborn among many brethren. Moreover whom he did predestinate, them he also called: and whom he called, them he also justified: and whom he justified, them he also glorified.

To accept Calvin's position, we would have to translate this verse to say, "Whom he did unconditionally elect, he also unconditionally elected."

Jesus said in Revelation 22:13:

> I am Alpha and Omega, the beginning and the end, the first and the last.

Obviously then, He knows the beginning and the end. Simply put, God knows everything! You don't have to make something spooky about the subject of God's foreknowledge, unless you are a Calvinist trying to support Calvinism. God, in His foreknowledge, knows who will trust Jesus Christ as Savior; however, that does not mean He has to make the decision for them to be saved.

SALVATION IS OFFERED TO ALL

As mentioned earlier, Revelation 22:17 says:

> And the Spirit and the bride say, Come. And let him that heareth say, Come. And let him that is athirst come. And whosoever will, let him take the water of life freely.

Romans 10:13 says:

> For whosoever shall call upon the name of the Lord shall be saved.

Titus 2:11 says:

> For the grace of God that bringeth salvation hath appeared to *all* men. (emphasis added)

Why would the grace of God appear to all men if most of them are already and very decidedly doomed to Hell, and there is nothing they can do about it? Is God dangling a "carrot" of salvation in front of all men, only to yank it away and send most of them to Hell, whether they would have chosen that salvation or not? What a morbid view of God. And an unbiblical one!

John 12:32 says:

> And I, if I be lifted up from the earth, will draw *all* men unto me. (emphasis added)

As mentioned earlier in this chapter, 2 Peter 3:9 tells us:

> The Lord is not slack concerning his promise, as some men count slackness; but is longsuffering to us-ward, not willing that *any* should perish, but that all should come to repentance. (emphasis added)

Romans 5:12 says:

. . . all have sinned.

Acts 17:30 says:

God . . . commandeth all men every where to repent.

Why would God command all men to repent (i.e., be saved) if He knew they had no control in the matter, and He was already decided in sending most of them to Hell?

WHO WILL YOU BELIEVE?

Contrary to John Calvin's heresy, you are free to choose!

TO TEACH THAT GOD'S LOVE IS LIMITED IS TO TEACH HERESY

The basic Calvinist theory of limited atonement is that the death of Christ on Calvary's cross was limited for only those whom they call the "elect." This means it would be impossible to tell a sinner who was not one of their so-called elect that Christ died for him or her. The teaching of Calvin concerning limited atonement means that God ordained some people for Heaven and ordained the rest to suffer in Hell for eternity. This is a wicked attack on the character of God who tells us in many verses in the Bible that Christ died for everyone!

First John 2:2 tells us:

[Christ] is the propitiation for our sins: and not for ours only, but also for the sins of the whole world.

To use the Calvinist "solution" to support Calvinism by changing the word "world" to "elect," this verse would read, "Christ is the propitiation for the elect's sins: and not for the elect's only, but also for the sins of the elect." First Timothy 2:6 plainly says Christ "gave himself a ransom for all." All means all!

THE WORD "WORLD" MEANS WORLD

John 1:29 says:

> Behold the Lamb of God, which taketh away the sin of the world.

John 3:16 says:

> For God so loved the world, that he gave his only begotten Son, that whosoever believeth in him should not perish, but have everlasting life.

As previously mentioned, A. W. Pink says:

> The "world" in John 3:16 must, in the final analysis, refer to the world of God's people. Must we say, for there is no alternative solution.*

The only "solution" for a Calvinist, if he is going to support his heresy with Scripture, is to change the meaning of words in the Scriptures.

John 3:17 says:

* On page 26.

For God sent not his Son into the world to condemn the world; but that the world through him might be saved.

It does not say, God sent not his Son unto the elect to condemn the elect, that the elect through him might be saved.

First John 2:2 says:

And he is the propitiation for our sins: and not for ours only, but also for the sins of the whole world.

The term used in the Bible—"the whole world"—is not ambiguous nor is it difficult to understand.

First John 4:14 says:

And we have seen and do testify that the Father sent the Son to be the Saviour of the world.

TO TEACH WE DO NOT HAVE THE ABILITY TO CHOOSE OR REFUSE IS TO TEACH HERESY

MAN CAN CHOOSE

[T]hey have chosen their own ways, and their soul delighteth in their abominations. . . . [T]hey did evil before mine eyes, and chose that in which I delighted not. (Isaiah 66:3, 4)

Choosing rather to suffer affliction. (Hebrews 11:25)

[C]hoose you this day whom ye will serve. (Joshua 24:15)

[They] did not choose the fear of the LORD. (Proverbs 1:29)

[C]hoose life, that both thou and thy see may life. (Deuteronomy 30:19)

Let Your hand be ready to help me, For I have chosen Your precepts. (Psalm 119:173)

To day if ye will hear his voice, harden not your hearts, as in the provocation. (Hebrews 3:15)

The word "choose" is in the Bible over sixty times, and the word *always* means choose. Groups like Calvinism can only survive when they say the Bible is saying something different than it *is* saying. Like the saying goes, "When the plain sense of Scripture makes common sense seek no other sense lest it all become nonsense."

MAN CAN REFUSE

. . . refused to obey. (Nehemiah 9:17)

. . . refused to walk in his law. (Psalm 78:10)

I have called, and ye refused. (Proverbs 1:24)

. . . refused to hear. (Jeremiah 11:9-10)

. . . refused to hearken. (Zechariah 7:11)

. . . refused to be comforted.—Jacob (Genesis 37:35)

[T]he people refused to obey. (1 Samuel 8:19)

. . . refused to walk in his law. (Psalm 78:10)

I have called, and ye refused. (Proverbs 1:24)

See that ye refuse not him that speaketh. (Hebrews 12:25)

Moses . . . refused to be called the son of Pharaoh's daughter. (Hebrews 11:24)

The words "refuse" or "refused" are found in the Bible over fifty times. To suggest the Bible teaches that man does not have the ability to make decisions is foolish. If God has not given man a free will, what kind of head games do Calvinist teachers think God is playing with people?

CALVINISTS TEACH WE DO NOT HAVE THE ABILITY TO BELIEVE VERSES ON BELIEVING

. . . even to them that believe on his name. (John 1:12)

But these are written, that ye might believe. (John 20:31)

. . . that believing ye might have life. (John 20:31)

. . . them that believe. (1 Corinthians 1:21)

. . . them that believe. (Hebrews 10:39)

He that believeth on him is not condemned: but he that believeth not is condemned already, because he hath not believed in the name of the only begotten Son of God. (John 3:18)

. . . he that believeth not God hath made him a liar; because he believeth not the record that God gave of his Son. (1 John 5:10)

Jesus never preached saying, "I am going to die for some of you, and the rest of you only came into the world so my Father could be glorified in sending you to Hell."

CALVINISTS TEACH THAT GOD'S GRACE IS IRRESISTIBLE

Psalm 78:22 says God's anger was kindled, "Because they believed not in God, and trusted not in his salvation."

Psalm 78:32 says, "they sinned still, and believed not."

Psalm 106:24 says, "they believed not his word."

John 12:37 says, "yet they believed not on him."

Acts 17:5 tell of, "the Jews which believed not."

Acts 19:9 says some, "were hardened, and believed not."

Acts 28:24 says, "And some believed the things which were spoken, and some believed not."

According to these verses and many others, people *have* resisted and are *able* to resist the grace of God. If the Calvinist view that man cannot resist God's grace is true, then this takes all responsibility off man if he *does* resist (i.e., the non-elect) because he has no control either way, and how can God send those not responsible for resisting to eternal damnation?

MAN'S FREE WILL IS ACCORDING TO GOD'S GOOD PLEASURE

Remember, the sovereignty of God simply means, God's "absolute right to do all things according to his own good pleasure."* Ephesians 1:5 says:

Having predestinated us unto the adoption of children by Jesus Christ to himself, according to the good pleasure of his will.

Notice that it says He adopts us as "children." Children have a free will, and that is why they need to be trained—so they can make the right choices.

---

* See page 26.

The Bible is very plain that it was, "according to the good pleasure of his will" to give man a free will; and in so doing, it *did not* interfere with His sovereignty. Actually, the fact that God gave man free will is greater proof of God's sovereignty than if God made only robot-like people. Though God knew that free will would enable man to choose to reject Him, it would also bring Him pleasure in having created beings who freely respond to His love with a love for Him that is not programmed or forced but is truly heart-felt in each individual.

His good will here deals with the plan of salvation. It is "by Jesus Christ." Acts 4:12 says:

> Neither is there salvation in any other: for there is none other name under heaven given among men, whereby we must be saved.

Ephesians 1:5 is not referring to *who* will be saved but rather *how* they will be saved.

Acts 10:34 plainly says, "God is no respecter of persons."

First Timothy 2:4 says God wants "all men to be saved, and to come unto the knowledge of the truth." First Timothy 2:6 tells us that Christ "gave himself a ransom for all."

A CONTRADICTION OF TERMS

The very title of "Irresistible Grace" is an oxymoron—a contradiction of terms. If it is irresistible, it is not grace. It would then be part of our human constitution or construction; in short, we *would* be robots. Proverbs 1:24-25 says:

> Because I have called, and ye refused; I have stretched out my hand, and no man regarded; But ye have set at nought all my counsel, and would none of my reproof.

God called, and man ignored Him. God stretched out His hand, and no man regarded. His counsels were refused as were His reproofs.

Numbers 14:18 says:

> The LORD is longsuffering.

Psalm 103:8 says:

> The LORD is merciful and gracious, slow to anger, and plenteous in mercy.

Acts 7:51 says:

> Ye stiffnecked and uncircumcised in heart and ears, ye do always resist the Holy Ghost: as your fathers did, so do ye.

Perhaps, before Calvinists build an entire doctrine on words not found in the Bible, they should check a dictionary for the meaning of the words they decide to use. Irresistible means, "impossible to resist" (*Webster*). Proverbs 29:1 states:

> He, that being often reproved hardeneth his neck, shall suddenly be destroyed, and that without remedy.

God's justice requires being reproved once. God's grace is man reproved over and over again, which also means man resisted over and over again. Again, Proverbs 1:24 says:

> Because I have called, and ye refused; I have stretched out my hand, and no man regarded.

John 5:40 warns:

> [Y]e will not come to me, that ye might have life.

To be scripturally correct, if Calvinist teachers want to build a doctrine by putting a word in front of the word "grace," they will have to call it "Resistible Grace." There is not one passage of Scripture from Genesis to Revelation that teaches that God's grace is irresistibly bestowed on anyone. God forces nobody to get saved.

GOD FORCES NOBODY TO BELIEVE

[T]hey believed not his word. (Psalm 106:24)

. . . some of you that believe not. (John 6:64)

[Y]e believed not. (John 10:25)

. . . yet they believed not on him. (John 12:37)

. . . believed not. (Acts 9:26)

. . . the Jews which believed not. (Acts 17:5)

. . . were hardened, and believed not. (Acts 19:9)

. . . believed not the truth. (2 Thessalonians 2:12)

. . . them that believed not. (Hebrews 11:31)

. . . them that believed not. (Jude 1:5)

And some believed the things which were spoken, and some believed not. (Acts 28:24)

7

CALVINISM'S PERSEVERANCE

THE WORD PERSEVERANCE IS FOUND ONLY once in the Scriptures. Ephesians 6:18 commands the believer to be, "Praying always with all prayer and supplication in the Spirit, and watching thereunto with all perseverance and supplication for all saints." This verse is speaking of perseverance in prayer and has nothing to do with persevering unto salvation. The dictionary meaning as well as the meaning of the Greek word here is to hold to or adhere to a course of action.[1]

CALVIN'S PERSEVERANCE IS *NOT* ETERNAL SECURITY

Many Christians wrongly assume that the Calvinist theory of "the perseverance of the saints" is synonymous with the doctrine of eternal security. The biblical doctrine of eternal security teaches that one who has been truly saved by God's grace is kept eternally saved by God's grace. God has not left our eternal destiny in our ability to persevere. For God to do that would result in a salvation by works.

Citing Augustine, Calvin wrote, "[T]hose who do not persevere unto the end belong not to the calling of God."[2]

Calvin also stated:

> [W]hat they [the Christians at Corinth] had attained so far is nothing, unless they keep steadily on; because it is not enough that they once started off on the way of the Lord, if they do not make an effort to reach the goal.[3]

In A. W. Pink's book *Practical Christianity*, Pink taught, "[I]f there is a reserve in your obedience, you are on the road to hell."[4]

Pink also said:

> Something more than believing in Christ is necessary to ensure the soul's reaching Heaven.[5]

Reformed minister John Otis states that, "maintaining an unforgiving spirit . . . will surely destroy our souls in hell."[6]

In his book, *The Doctrine of Sanctification*, A. W. Pink stated:

> [H]oliness in this life is such a part of our "salvation" that it is a *necessary means* to make us meet

to be partakers of the inheritance of the saints in heavenly light and glory.[7]

Calvinist theologian and co-founder of the Westminster Theological Seminary, Dr. John Murray states:

[L]et us appreciate the doctrine of the perseverance of the saints and recognize that we may entertain the faith of our security in Christ only as we persevere in faith and holiness to the end.[8]

DID THE MAN GOD USED TO WRITE OVER FIFTY CHAPTERS OF THE BIBLE NOT PERSEVERE?

For it came to pass, when Solomon was old, that his wives turned away his heart after other gods . . . his heart was turned from the LORD God of Israel . . . he kept not that which the LORD commanded. (1 Kings 11:4,9,10)

The man whom God used to write Proverbs, Ecclesiastes, and the Song of Solomon turned away from God into idolatry and apostasy.

As noted, A. W. Pink said, "If there is a reserve in your obedience, you are on the road to hell." How do Calvinists put this all together? Would they have us believe God predestined an unsaved (non-elect) man to write Proverbs, Ecclesiastes, and the Song of Solomon and then when He was finished with him sent him to Hell?

WHAT ABOUT SAINTS WHO DIDN'T PERSEVERE?

First Corinthians 1:2 tells us this letter was written, "Unto the church." It says they were "saints." How does Calvin's perseverance of the saints fit in with these saints God repeatedly referred to as "carnal"?

First Corinthians 5:13 commands the saints at the local church in Corinth to, "put away from among yourselves that wicked person." The fact that they were not dealing with sin in their church is an example of the saints not persevering because the whole church was guilty of not dealing with a serious matter.

In the seven churches in Revelation, only one was found acceptable. By Calvin's guidelines, the members of all these churches were going to Hell.

The Bible has many specific examples of believers who did not persevere according to John Calvin's theory.

Noah got drunk, Abraham was a liar, Jacob schemed, Sampson failed, David fell into sin and was responsible for the death of a man, Moses didn't follow God's instructions and was not allowed to enter the *promised land*, John Mark quit, Peter cursed and denied Christ, and all the disciples forsook Jesus. The list goes on and on. Yet, A. W. Pink said, "If there is a reserve in your obedience, you are on the road to hell," That means all these people were on the road to Hell! And where does that leave us?

There is actually *no* eternal security in the doctrine of the "perseverance of the saints" because no one can ever know—even at the end of his life—if he had really persevered *enough*. And from a biblical standpoint, saints persevering for salvation are on extremely dangerous ground; as the apostle Paul points out, if you are depending on your works, works will not save you.

> Knowing that a man is not justified by the works of the law, but by the faith of Jesus Christ, even we have believed in Jesus Christ, that we might be justified by the faith of Christ, and not by the works of the law: for by the works of the law shall no flesh be justified. . . .
>
> I do not frustrate the grace of God: for if righteousness come by the law, then Christ is dead in vain. (Galatians 2:16, 21)

Calvinists believe the "perseverance of the saints" (the P in TULIP) offers them eternal security, but in actuality, it brings them more insecurity than ever regarding their salvation. Here, the persevering is left up to the strength of the believer rather than resting on the promises of God that assure us eternal life is based on what *He* has already done, not what we do. It is our part to believe, repent, and put our trust in Him and His part to save and preserve us.

Eternal security does not give believers permission to sin any more than the fathers of the faith, who stumbled, had an excuse for their sins and failures. However, the wonder of the Cross is that our sins are fully paid for—paid in full. Jesus said, "It is finished." Our redemption has been entirely purchased. We can rest in the assurance of salvation that the Gospel offers, as expressed by the apostles and prophets. But Calvinism, while it claims to be wholly dependent on the grace of God for salvation, has actually turned everything upside down with the teaching of the "perseverance of the saints," making salvation a works-based religion where grace is not truly grace. With Calvinism, the responsibility of salvation is put on the believer thereby nullifying grace altogether. Paul explained this when he said:

> And if by grace, then is it no more of works: otherwise grace is no more grace. But if it be of works, then it is no more grace: otherwise work is no more work. (Romans 11:6)

8

NO ASSURANCE
OF SALVATION

EVEN JOHN CALVIN HIMSELF DID NOT possess assurance of salvation. Writing in his will shortly before his death in 1564, he declared:

> I testify also and profess that I humbly seek from God, _that He may so will me_ to be washed and purified by the great Redeemer's blood, s*hed for the sins of the human race,* that it may be permitted me to stand before His tribunal under the covert of the Redeemer Himself.[1] (italics in original; underline added)

John 3:36 says:

He that believeth on the Son hath everlasting life: and he that believeth not the Son shall not see life; but the wrath of God abideth on him.

Calvin taught that he could not believe unless God first regenerated him and gave him faith to believe. It is not surprising, therefore, that Calvin or any Calvinist cannot have an assurance of salvation and, therefore, he must adhere to his perseverance of the saints theory.

No Calvinist can be sure of his salvation because he might be predestined just to *think* he is saved. After all, playing little head games with people would not be wrong for Calvin's "God" since Calvin's "God" is glorified by sending billions of people who had no choice to Hell for eternity.

MORE CALVINISTS ON PERSEVERANCE

As I mentioned in the last chapter, Calvinist pastor John Murray says:

> [W]e may entertain the faith of our security in Christ only as we persevere in faith and holiness to the end.[2]

How much holiness? Are we talking about sinless perfection? Calvinist theologian Charles Hodge (1797-1878), in referring to evidence of being elected, said:

> The only evidence of election is effectual calling, that is, the production of holiness. And the only evidence of the genuineness of this call and the certainty of our perseverance, is a patient continuance in well doing.[3]

Again, John Murray stated:

> The perseverance of the saints reminds us very forcefully that only those who persevere to the end are truly saints.[4]

In the perseverance discussion, John MacArthur states that "you may be a spiritual defector who hasn't defected yet."[5]

"I WAS TERRIFIED!"

In an article titled "Assurance of Salvation," the highly popular Calvinist teacher, the late R. C. Sproul (d. 2017) wrote:

> A while back I had one of those moments . . . suddenly the question hit me: "R. C., what if you are not one of the redeemed? What if your destiny is not heaven after all, but hell?" Let me tell you that I was flooded in my body with a chill that went from my head to the bottom of my spine. I was terrified.[6]

There is not a person in the world who believes what John Calvin taught who should *not* be terrified concerning the reality of his salvation.

Sproul continued:

> I began to take stock of my life, and I looked at my performance. My sins came pouring into my mind, and the more I looked at myself the worse I felt. I thought, "Maybe it's really true. Maybe

I'm not saved after all." . . . Then I remembered John 6:68. Jesus had been giving out hard teaching, and many of His former followers had left Him. When He asked Peter if he was also going to leave, Peter said, "Where else can we go? Only You have words of eternal life." In other words, Peter was also uncomfortable, but he realized that being uncomfortable with Jesus was better than any other option.[7]

Uncomfortable with Jesus? This doesn't line up with Scripture that promises peace with God and eternal life to those who believe in Jesus Christ and accept His sacrifice on the Cross as a penalty for their sins. Consider these passages:

> Therefore being justified by faith, we have peace with God through our Lord Jesus Christ. (Romans 5:1)

> And this is the promise that he hath promised us, even eternal life. (1 John 2:25)

> And this is the record, that God hath given to us eternal life, and this life is in his Son. (1 John 5:11)

> These things have I written unto you that believe on the name of the Son of God; that ye may know that ye have eternal life. (1 John 5:13)

A. W. Pink's "solution" for supporting Calvinism is to change the meaning of words to support his theory; Sproul's "option" is to be "uncomfortable with Jesus," which he considered "better than any other option." It is very difficult to understand why any Christian with a basic understanding of the Scriptures would accept another gospel that is not only heretical and very dangerous but strips a believer of the assurance and peace that the Scriptures promise to "whosoever will."

CALVIN TAUGHT THAT GOD ORDAINED ADAM TO SIN

Calvin said:

> The Fall of Adam was not by accident, nor by chance, but was ordained by the secret counsel of God.[8]

He also said that,

> The first man fell because the Lord deemed it meet that he should.[9]

OTHER CALVINISTS TEACH THAT GOD ORDAINED SIN

In Edwin Palmer's book, *The Five Points of Calvinism,* he states:

> God is in back of everything. He decides and causes all things to happen that do happen . . . even sin. . . . God ordained sin and unbelief.[10]

Loraine Boettner, who embraced Calvinistic beliefs while studying at Princeton in the 1920s, said that God "creates the very thoughts and intents of the soul."[11] R. C. Sproul Jr. (R. C. Sproul's Calvinist son) said that God "desired that man would fall into sin . . . [God] created sin."[12] And A. W. Pink said, "[God] foreordained sin should enter the world."[13] Isn't it rather shocking that scholars will demonstrate such ignorance of the nature and character of God? John said in his epistle, "God is light, and in him is no darkness at all" (1 John 1:5). In other words, there is not even an iota of iniquity with God. It is blasphemous to say God is the author of sin or has any part with sin (see Romans 3:8).

9

THINK IT THROUGH!

ACCORDING TO CALVINISM'S STANDARD that God is in "back of everything," God preordained (and wanted) David to commit adultery. Yet, Deuteronomy 5:21 says man should not "desire thy neighbour's wife," so how could God ordain or plan for David to desire his neighbor's wife? And if this picture of God is true, then He desired people to be, "Backbiters, haters of God, despiteful, proud, boasters, inventors of evil things, disobedient to their parents" as listed in Romans 1:30.

And if Calvinism is right, then God desired the rapists in Genesis 19:5 to come in an attempt to abuse the angels that visited Lot. And God desired Amnon to rape his sister in 2 Samuel 13:2.

According to Calvinism, God desired every child that has ever been molested to be abused. He desired every person murdered to be murdered. He desired every sin that was ever committed to be committed.

If that is not heresy, what does one have to teach in order for it to be heresy?

The title of this book, *Calvinism: None Dare Call It Heresy,* may seem too strong to some in that it is calling Calvinism heresy. But after reading the quotes as well as the Scripture verses I have presented to you, should anyone question why we refer to Calvinism as heresy?

The word heresy, from a Christian point of view, means to deviate or dissent from the fundamentals of biblical faith (i.e., the salvation message). If Calvinism has not veered from the biblical Gospel message, I don't know what has—it portrays a monster "God" who created billions of people whom he hates, whom he has given no choice in rejecting or accepting him, but whom He will send to eternal damnation anyway. Tragically, many who have believed in this "God" who ordains sin and evil have left the faith altogether because they cannot believe in a "God" who is so filled with hate and evil. Calvinism is not just heresy, it is dangerous and pitiful heresy.

Pink and those who support Calvinism have wasted a lot of paper attempting to get around the fact that they are really saying God is the Author of sin. However, if God foreordained sin, He foreordained sin! The dictionary says to foreordain is to "appoint in advance." Any child who can read can understand what Calvin meant when he said, "the Fall of Adam was not by accident, nor by chance, but was ordained by the secret counsel of God."[1]

CAN A CHRISTIAN BE A HERETIC?

The only time the Bible uses the word heretic is when it is talking about a Christian. Titus 3:10 says, "A man that is an heretick after the first and second admonition reject." Chapter 1:13 says, ". . . rebuke them sharply, that they may be sound in the faith." Chapter two and three continue with order in the local church including the teaching of "sound doctrine."

Second Thessalonians 3:14-15 says:

> And if any man obey not our word by this epistle, note that man, and have no company with him, that he may be ashamed. Yet count him not as an enemy, but admonish him as a brother.

In Galatians 5:7, Paul says, "Ye did run well; who did hinder you that ye should not obey the truth?" He warns them of being guilty of works of the flesh and included in the list is "heresies" (v. 20).

HOW ARE WE TO DEAL WITH HERESY

The Bible instructs us to study the Scriptures that we might know the truth and might not be ashamed in what we believe.

> Study to shew thyself approved unto God, a workman that needeth not to be ashamed, rightly dividing the word of truth. (2 Timothy 2:15)

With regard to how we are to deal with heresies and those teaching them, Romans 16:17 says:

> Now I beseech you, brethren, mark them which cause divisions and offences contrary to the doctrine which ye have learned; and avoid them.

Dave Hunt, in *What Love is This?*, explains the importance of not ignoring false teachings and heresies:

> [T]he history of the church from its earliest beginnings has involved sharp differences of opinion on many vital subjects, including the gospel itself. Numerous destructive heresies have developed and have been vigorously opposed. Neither Christ nor His apostles considered divergent views on the essentials of the gospel to be normal or acceptable, but commanded the believers to "earnestly contend for the faith which was once delivered unto the saints" [Jude 1:3]. That command applies to us today.[2]

The Bible doesn't say, "don't worry about heresy when taught by your friends." It doesn't say, "allow them to infiltrate your churches and Bible colleges and teach their heresy."

10

IN CONCLUSION

THE MATERIAL I HAVE PRESENTED IN THIS book is not designed as an in-depth study but rather more of a primer to give a basic understanding of Calvinism. We must face the issue of Calvinism because it destroys some of the most important tenets of biblical Christianity including God's love, mercy, justice, and the Gospel itself. In essence, Calvinism presents "another gospel."

There are some Calvinists who will argue that we have misrepresented Calvinism. One problem is some people are Calvin Calvinists, others are Thomas Fuller Calvinists, Arthur W. Pink Calvinists, Presbyterian Calvinists, Baptist Calvinists, MacArthur Calvinists, and so forth. It would be difficult not to misrepresent somebody's version of Calvinism.

Many people who call themselves Calvinists have never read Calvin's *Institutes of Christian Religion* for themselves. They are merely following someone who taught them something about his own brand of Calvinism. Some preachers have taken a few classes on Calvinism in a Bible college and then spend the rest of their lives supporting it because they liked the professor who presented it.

Some Calvinists call themselves three- or four-point Calvinists. That is about as erroneous as calling yourself a two-point Catholic because Catholics believe what the Bible says about the virgin birth and are against abortion.

To those Calvinist supporters who may be upset concerning any of my statements in this book, you should not be upset, because if Calvinism is right, I was foreordained by God to write it all.

APPENDIX I

SHOULD CHRISTIANS EXPOSE ERROR?

By Harry A. Ironside

OBJECTION IS OFTEN RAISED—EVEN BY SOME sound in the faith—regarding the exposure of error as being entirely negative and of no real edification. Of late, the hue and cry has been against any and all negative teaching. But the brethren who assume this attitude forget that a large part of the New Testament, both of the teaching of our blessed Lord Himself and the writings of the apostles, is made up of this very character of ministry—namely, showing the Satanic origin and, therefore, the unsettling results of the propagation of erroneous systems which Peter, in his second epistle, so definitely refers to as "damnable heresies."

Our Lord prophesied, "Many false prophets shall rise, and shall deceive many." Within our own day, how many false prophets have risen; and oh, how many are the deceived! Paul predicted:

> I know this, that after my departing shall grievous wolves enter in among you, not sparing the flock. Also of your own selves shall men arise, speaking perverse things, to draw away disciples after them. Therefore watch. (Acts 20:29-31)

My own observation is that these "grievous wolves," alone and in packs, are not sparing even the most favored flocks. Undershepherds in these "perilous times" will do well to note the apostle's warning:

> Take heed therefore unto yourselves, and to all the flock, over the which the Holy Ghost hath made you overseers. (v. 28)

It is as important in these days as in Paul's—in fact, it is increasingly important—to expose the many types of false teaching that, on every hand, abound more and more.

We are called upon to "earnestly contend for the faith which was once delivered unto the saints" (Jude 1:3), while we hold the truth in love. The faith means the whole body of revealed truth, and to contend for all of God's truth necessitates some negative teaching. The choice is not left with us. Jude said he preferred a different, a pleasanter theme:

> Beloved, when I gave all diligence to write unto you of the common salvation, it was needful for me to write unto you, and exhort you that ye should earnestly contend for the faith which was once delivered unto the saints. For there are certain men crept in unawares, who were before of old ordained to this condemnation, ungodly men, turning the grace of our God into lasciviousness, and denying the only Lord God, and our Lord Jesus Christ. (Jude 1:3-4)

Paul, likewise, admonishes us to "have no fellowship with the unfruitful works of darkness, but rather reprove them" (Ephesians 5:11).

This does not imply harsh treatment of those entrapped by error—quite the opposite. If it be objected that exposure to error necessitates unkind reflection upon others who do not see as we do, our answer is: it has always been the duty of every loyal servant of Christ to warn against any teaching that would make Him less precious or cast reflection upon His finished redemptive work and the all-sufficiency of His present service as our great High Priest and Advocate.

Every system of teaching can be judged by what it sets forth as to these fundamental truths of the faith. "What think ye of Christ?" is still the true test of every creed. The Christ of the Bible is certainly not the Christ of any false "-ism." Each of the cults has its hideous caricature of our lovely Lord.

Let us who have been redeemed at the cost of His precious blood be "good soldiers of Jesus Christ." As the battle against the forces of evil waxes ever more hot, we have need for God-given valor.

There is constant temptation to compromise. "Let us go forth therefore unto Him without the camp, bearing his reproach" (Hebrews 13:13). It is always right to stand firmly for what God has revealed concerning His blessed Son's person and work. The "father of lies" deals in half-truths and specializes in most subtle fallacies concerning the Lord Jesus, our sole and sufficient Savior.

Error is like leaven of which we read, "A little leaven leaveneth the whole lump" (Galatians 5:9). Truth mixed with error is equivalent to all error, except that it is more innocent looking and, therefore, more dangerous. God hates such a mixture! Any error, or any truth-and-error mixture, calls for definite exposure and repudiation. To condone such is to be unfaithful to God and His Word and treacherous to imperiled souls for whom Christ died.

Exposing error is most unpopular work. But from every true standpoint it is worthwhile work. To our Savior, it means that He receives from us, His blood-bought ones, the loyalty that is His due. To ourselves, if we consider "the reproach of Christ greater riches than the treasures of Egypt," it ensures future reward, a thousand-fold. And to souls "caught in the snare of the fowler," how many of them God only knows, it may mean light and life, abundant and everlasting.[1]

APPENDIX II

A BIBLICAL PERSPECTIVE ON SALVATION

NO SUBJECT EVER DISCUSSED CAN BE MORE important and crucial in this life than the subject of salvation. This is what the citizens of Berea were discussing where it says in Acts 17:11, "they received the word with all readiness of mind, and searched the scriptures daily, whether those things were so." The Bereans did two things right here in that their humble disposition motivated them with "readiness" to receive instruction, and they went to the Scriptures as the final authority on the subject. Notice the plural word "scriptures" is used as it is essential that Scripture be compared with Scripture in order to find out if "those things were so."

Although this may sound elementary (and it actually is) the sad reality is that human nature (in particular our sin nature) tends to be impulsive, and it is so easy to grab one verse, or maybe just one or two words, from the Bible and run with it, twisting and distorting it from its actual meaning in Scripture. For example, Jesus referred to himself as "the bread of life" (John 6:35), which was obviously a figure of speech. However, Jesus then emphasized the point by saying, "For my flesh is meat indeed, and my blood is drink indeed . . . he that eateth me, even he shall live by me" (John 6:55,57). Even though Jesus then qualified His statement by saying, "This is that bread which came down from heaven" (John 6:58), comparing Himself with manna, His disciples were already locked into a confusion, disputing amongst themselves what He could mean by His statements. The fact is, from a non-figurative perspective, partaking of human flesh was an unthinkable abomination, and the partaking of any kind of blood was forbidden in the Law.

For the reason of their great confusion, Jesus later explained to His disciples that (a) He would soon ascend to Heaven (John 6:62) making all He had said impossible in a physical sense, (b) that partaking of flesh "profiteth nothing" (John 6:63), and (c) the words He had spoken, "they are spirit" (John 6:63) (i.e., a figure of speech). Then, at the Last Supper, Jesus made it even clearer that He had been using a figure of speech by referring to the bread and wine as His body and blood (which obviously was impossible in a literal sense because He was still physically present) and then saying, "this do in remembrance of me" (Luke 22:19) to signify that they were to remember His sacrifice on the Cross in this manner. Most unfortunately, the Catholic Church has turned this memorial into a very literal "sacrament of the Eucharist" where participation in this sacrament is what saves you. Hence, we now have "another gospel" that is works based and therefore never for certain.

Likewise, John Calvin did much the same thing, except in his case, he latched onto little more than a single word (predestinate) and ran with it. Then, rather than carefully looking to the whole of Scripture to verify his precepts and conclusions, he looked to the writings of Augustine to verify his thinking. The result is that, as with Catholicism, we now have "another gospel" that is not solely based on Scripture but on the confused thinking and misconstrued assumptions of a mere man.

With Calvin, rather than changing his views to fit Scripture, he changed the meaning of words in Scripture to fit his now distorted view of God and salvation.

We will, therefore, look to Scripture on the subjects pertaining to salvation. A good place to start is chapter 33 of Ezekiel where the very words of God, spoken through a prophet, reveal God's heart on the subject of repentance:

> Again, the word of the LORD came unto me, saying . . .
>
> So thou, O son of man, I have set thee a watchman unto the house of Israel; therefore thou shalt hear the word at my mouth, and *warn them* from me. . . .
>
> Say unto them, As I live, saith the Lord God, I have *no pleasure* in the death of the wicked; but

that the wicked turn from his way and live: turn ye, turn ye from your evil ways; for *why will ye* die, O house of Israel? . . .

[A]s for the wickedness of the wicked, he shall not fall thereby *in the day that he turneth from his wickedness* . . . When I shall say to the righteous, *that he shall surely live*; if he trust to his *own righteousness*, and commit iniquity, all his righteousnesses shall not be remembered . . .

Yet the children of thy people say, The way of the Lord is not equal: but as for them, *their way is not equal.* When the righteous turneth from his righteousness, and committeth iniquity, he shall even die thereby. But if the wicked turn from his wickedness, and do that which is lawful and right, he shall live thereby. Yet ye say, The way of the Lord is not equal. O ye house of Israel, *I will judge you every one after his ways.* (Ezekiel 33:1,7,11-13,17-20; emphasis added)

For the sake of brevity, we have hopped from verse to verse in Ezekiel 33, but if you have suffered under the teaching of Calvinism, it would do you well to carefully read *all* of this portion of Scripture through the twentieth verse as this passage refutes Calvinism without Calvinists doing some very serious mental gymnastics in altering and twisting the meaning of words. The italicized portions especially reveal that:

- God has given everyone a free will.

- Everyone already has the God-given ability to choose whether or not to live for God.

- Our destiny—Heaven or Hell—is our choice, but if we choose Heaven, we must choose to do it God's way as we cannot trust (i.e., be saved) in our own righteousness.

- God takes no pleasure in sending people to Hell. It is not His choice but our choice to make.

- God is "equal" in His dealings with all of mankind. He is not a cruel or unjust God. It is those who depict God as cruel and unjust (as one who delights in sending people to Hell) who are "not equal"—or perhaps it is better to say blasphemous. Even the apostle Peter said that God is "no respecter of persons" (Acts 10:34), and Paul said, "there is no respect of persons with God" (Romans 2:11). (See also Ephesians 6:9 and Colossians 3:25.) In other words, both Peter and Paul are in agreement with Ezekiel in that God is equal and fair in His dealings with all people. But John Calvin opposed this truth in saying, "All are not created on equal terms, but some are preordained to eternal life, others to eternal damnation."[1]

- Repentance is a pre-conversion experience. It precedes the grace (indwelling Holy Spirit) that God gives to live a godly life.

Next, let's consider the ministry of John the Baptist. Jesus said of him, "Among those that are born of women there is not a greater prophet than John the Baptist: but he that is least in the kingdom of God is greater than he" (Luke 7:28). Scripture also says of him, "Behold, I send my messenger before thy face, which shall prepare thy way before thee [Jesus] . . . John did baptize in the wilderness, and preach the baptism of repentance for the remission of sins" (Mark 1:2,4). Though the religious leaders stayed away, many unconverted sinners came to John and partook of this baptism of repentance. As is indicated here, historically they repented as a prelude to later receiving Christ as their Savior. John the Baptist said of Jesus, "I indeed baptize you with water; but . . . he shall baptize you with the Holy Ghost and with fire" (Luke 3:16). But, while these people were yet sinners, God made repentance available to all who willed it through the ministry of John the Baptist.

Then in Acts 16:30, the Philippian jailer asks of Paul and Silas, "Sirs, what must I do to be saved?" to which they respond, "Believe on the Lord Jesus Christ, and thou shalt be saved, and thy house" (Acts 16:31).

For the Calvinist, any testimony of a conversion experience may be questioned and scrutinized. In fact, except for this being in Scripture, they would tell you that such a testimony is totally unacceptable. From a fatalistic, predestinate viewpoint, neither the jailer nor his family could have any choice in the matter, so most likely they would all go to Hell. Also, beyond their lacking any free will in the matter, they are fully degenerate to the degree that they are unable to repent or believe. Such is the predicament for the Calvinist who is fully indoctrinated into Calvin's teachings. It is a large pill to swallow, and it is to be swallowed whole.

From a biblical perspective, the conversion experience is not forced or manipulated but initiated of a person's own free will as the Holy Spirit draws him (remember John 12:32 where Jesus says He will draw *all* men). The individual repents and believes, then is "born again" of the Holy Spirit. From the Calvinist perspective, one must be born again first before one can repent and believe, but this is Scripture turned upside down and backwards.

Perhaps the act of becoming a Christian can best be explained by illustration: It is like a person walking down the wrong path; the person then stops and turns around (repentance), then looks to the right direction (faith). (This is what God requires to be born again.) To be born again means to be indwelt with the Holy Spirit as Paul indicates that Christians have God's Spirit in them (Romans 8:9).Now with the Holy Spirit abiding within, the person begins walking in the new direction. It should be noted here that biblical repentance does not mean that we must clean up our act before we can come to Christ. Rather, it is an admission of our guilt and of our need of a Savior to begin transforming our lives to the image of God's Son. Walking in the new direction, then, is subsequent to first repenting and believing. Then, as we will never be perfect in this life, we will continue to live a life of faith and repentance as the Holy Spirit continually transforms us to be like the Son.

In conclusion, it is important to realize that we will never understand all of Scripture perfectly, but the fundamentals of the Gospel can be readily comprehended. God is love and will not turn away whosoever comes to Him. Unfortunately, many come to Calvinism because on the surface, it appears to offer comfort and assurance of salvation. But, like Catholicism, there is no real assurance of salvation in Calvinism where salvation is deemed to be predestinated and therefore inaccessible by our choice or will. Once fully indoctrinated into Calvinism, the Calvinist is left wondering for the rest of his life if he is one of the elect. This is not a walk of faith but of doubt, and it is totally unscriptural. Scripture says that we can walk in assurance of eternal life:

> *Whosoever believeth* that Jesus is the Christ *is born of God.* (1 John 5:1; emphasis added)

> And the Spirit and the bride say, *Come.* And *let him* that heareth say, *Come.* And *let him* that is athirst *come.* And *whosoever will, let him take* the water of life *freely.* (Revelation 22:17; emphasis added)

> These things have I written unto you that believe on the name of the Son of God; *that ye may know* that ye have eternal life, and that ye may believe on the name of the Son of God. (1 John 5:13; emphasis added)

APPENDIX III

A BIBLICAL PERSPECTIVE ON CONTENDING FOR THE FAITH

For the word of God is quick, and powerful, and sharper than any twoedged sword, piercing even to the dividing asunder of soul and spirit, and of the joints and marrow, and is a discerner of the thoughts and intents of the heart. (Hebrews 4:12)

HOW DOES A BELIEVER RIGHTFULLY AND IN a godly manner (following the example of Jesus, Paul, and the disciples) deal with those who are bringing false teachings into the church.

In thinking about following the example of Jesus, the disciples, and Paul, there are verses from Scripture that help us outline a biblical guideline for both showing love and respect to others, while at the same time dealing biblically and godly with those bringing heretical doctrines into the church.

While we don't believe the New Testament condones cruel or hateful behavior to anyone, we do see a consistent pattern in Scripture that does not look lightly upon those who are teaching heretical doctrines or practices. Let us heed the whole counsel of God, which tells us to remain humble and in an attitude of grace (knowing we are not superior to others and that it is only by the grace of God that we can see these spiritual things), but also tells us to speak courageously, with confidence, honesty, and strength.

We are in a battle for the continuance of the Gospel message—souls are perishing—and words must be said. While we do care for the souls of the men and women who are bringing in dangerous false doctrine and practices, we cannot, in good conscience, take it lightly or have congenial "conversations" and futile private discussions.

> The night is far spent, the day is at hand: let us therefore cast off the works of darkness, and let us put on the armour of light. (Romans 13:12)

The Bible says that the message of the Cross is the power of God unto salvation (i.e., the doctrine of Christ—2 John 1:9-11). That is because it is the only way of salvation. When teachings and false doctrines threaten to diminish the "doctrine of Christ," it creates a very serious situation that cannot be handled "sitting down."

In view of this book about Calvinism that you have just read, consider these verses on how the Christian contender of the faith should speak and behave.

[B]e thou an example of the believers, in word, in conversation, in charity, in spirit, in faith, in purity. (1 Timothy 4:12)

. . . that we henceforth be no more children, tossed to and fro, and carried about with every wind of doctrine, by the sleight of men, and cunning craftiness, whereby they lie in wait to deceive; but speaking the truth in love, may grow up into him in all things, which is the head, even Christ. (Ephesians 4:14-15)

Wherefore putting away lying, speak every man truth with his neighbor. (Ephesians 4:25)

Let no corrupt communication proceed out of your mouth, but that which is good to the use of edifying, that it may minister grace unto the hearers. (Ephesians 4:29)

I . . . beseech you that ye walk worthy of the vocation wherewith ye are called, with all lowliness and meekness, with longsuffering, forbearing one another in love. (Ephesians 4:1-2)

Beware of false prophets, which come to you in sheep's clothing, but inwardly they are ravening wolves. (Matthew 7:15)

Brethren, if a man be overtaken in a fault, ye which are spiritual, restore such an one in the spirit of meekness; considering thyself, lest thou also be tempted. (Galatians 6:1)

But, beloved, remember ye the words which were spoken before of the apostles of our Lord Jesus Christ; how that they told you there should be mockers in the last time, who should walk after their own ungodly lusts. These be they who separate themselves, sensual, having not the Spirit. But ye, beloved, building up yourselves on your most holy faith, praying in the Holy Ghost, keep yourselves in the love of God, looking for the mercy of our Lord Jesus Christ unto eternal life. And of some have compassion, making a difference: and others save with fear, pulling them out of the fire; hating even the garment spotted by the flesh. (Jude 1:17-23)

A man that is an heretick after the first and second admonition reject, knowing that he that is such is subverted, and sinneth, being condemned of himself. (Titus 3:10-11)

But there were false prophets also among the people, even as there shall be false teachers among you, who privily shall bring in damnable heresies, even denying the Lord that bought them, and bring upon themselves swift destruction. And many shall follow their pernicious ways; by reason of whom the way of truth shall be evil spoken of. (2 Peter 2:1-2)

Now the works of the flesh are manifest, which are these; Adultery, fornication, uncleanness, lasciviousness, idolatry, witchcraft, hatred, variance, emulations, wrath, strife, seditions, heresies, envyings, murders, drunkenness, revellings, and such like: of the which I tell you before, as I have also told you in time past, that they which do such things shall not inherit the kingdom of God. (Galatians 5:19-21)

Whosoever transgresseth, and abideth not in the doctrine of Christ, hath not God. He that abideth in the doctrine of Christ, he hath both the Father and the Son. If there come any unto you, and bring not this doctrine, receive him not into your house, neither bid him God speed: For he that biddeth him God speed is partaker of his evil deeds. (2 John 1: 9-11)

Beloved, when I gave all diligence to write unto you of the common salvation, it was needful for me to write unto you, and exhort you that ye should earnestly contend for the faith which was once delivered unto the saints. For there are certain men crept in unawares, who were before of old ordained to this condemnation, ungodly men, turning the grace of our God into lasciviousness, and denying the only Lord God, and our Lord Jesus Christ. I will therefore put you in remembrance, though ye once knew this, how that the Lord, having saved the people out of the land of

Egypt, afterward destroyed them that believed not. (Jude 1:3-5)

I marvel that ye are so soon removed from him that called you into the grace of Christ unto another gospel: Which is not another; but there be some that trouble you, and would pervert the gospel of Christ. But though we, or an angel from heaven, preach any other gospel unto you than that which we have preached unto you, let him be accursed. As we said before, so say I now again, if any man preach any other gospel unto you than that ye have received, let him be accursed. For do I now persuade men, or God? or do I seek to please men? for if I yet pleased men, I should not be the servant of Christ. (Galatians 1:6-10)

I know thy works, and thy labour, and thy patience, and how thou canst not bear them which are evil: and thou hast tried them which say they are apostles, and are not, and hast found them liars: and hast borne, and hast patience, and for my name's sake hast laboured, and hast not fainted. (Revelation 2: 2-3)

. . . and that because of false brethren unawares brought in, who came in privily to spy out our liberty which we have in Christ Jesus, that they might bring us into bondage: To whom we gave place by subjection, no, not for an hour; that the truth of the gospel might continue with you. (Galatians 2: 4-5)

[Instructions to the disciples from Jesus before his death and resurrection]: Go your ways: behold, I send you forth as lambs among wolves. Carry neither purse, nor scrip, nor shoes: and salute no man by the way. And into whatsoever house ye enter, first say, Peace be to this house. And if the son of peace be there, your peace shall rest upon it: if not, it shall turn to you again. And in the same house remain, eating and drinking such things as they give: for the labourer is worthy of his hire. Go not from house to house. And into whatsoever city ye enter, and they receive you, eat such things as are set before you: and heal the sick that are therein, and say unto them, The kingdom of God is come nigh unto you. But into whatsoever city ye enter, and they receive you not, go your ways out into the streets of the same, and say, Even the very dust of your city, which cleaveth on us, we do wipe off against you: notwithstanding be ye sure of this, that the kingdom of God is come nigh unto you. But I say unto you, that it shall be more tolerable in that day for Sodom, than for that city. (Luke 10:3-12)[1]

ENDNOTES

INTRODUCTION

1.James Strong, *Strong's Concordance* (Grand Rapids, MI: Baker Books, 1982), p. 480. and Joseph H. Thayer, *Thayer's Greek/English Lexicon of the New Testament* (Grand Rapids, MI: Baker Books, 7th printing, 1982), p. 16. Also see at: https://www.blueletterbible.org/lang/Lexicon/Lexicon.cfm?strongs=G141&t=KJV.

2. John Calvin, *Institutes of the Christian Religion,* Vol. 3, (Orlando, Signalman Publishing, from the 4th edition, 2009, Kindle edition), Chapter 21, section 5, Kindle location 17221; also available at Christian Classics Ethereal Library (https://www.ccel.org/ccel/calvin/institutes.v.xxii.html).

CHAPTER 1: WHERE CALVIN GOT HIS THEOLOGY

1. John Calvin, *Concerning the Eternal Predestination of God* (Louisville, KY: Westminster John Knox Press edition, 1997), p. 63.

2. Stewart Sutherland, Leslie Houlden, Peter Clarke, and Friedhelm Hardy, *The World's Religions* (England, Routledge Companion Encyclopedias, 1988), p. 162.

3. Augustine, *The Writings Against the Manichaeans and Against the Donatists, Part II—The Donatists* (Devoted Pub-

Note: In some endnotes, the source material is taken from Kindle (e-book) editions. When page numbers are given along with Kindle location numbers, these are the page numbers provided by the Kindle edition.

lishing edition, 2017), p. 333; also available at Christian Classics Ethereal Library (https://www.ccel.org/ccel/schaff/npnf104.v.vi.viii.html).

4. Augustine, Edited by Philip Schaff, *A Treatise on the Merits and Forgiveness of Sins, and on the Baptism of Infants* (Aeterna Press, 2014 edition), p. 30.

5. Ibid., p. 29.

6. Ibid., p. 112.

7. Augustine, Edited by Philip Schaff, *A Treatise on the Merits and Forgiveness of Sins, and on the Baptism of Infants* (Kindle edition, published by Amazon Digital Services), Chapter 8, Kindle location 3350.

8. Augustine, *On Nature and Grace* (Pickerington, OH: Beloved Publishing, 2014), pp. 35-36.

9. For example, in *City of God* (Start Publishing e-edition 2012, Kindle edition), Augustine states on p. 533: ". . . it more evidently appears that some shall in the last judgment suffer some kind of purgatorial punishments."

10. Augustine, *Against the Fundamental Epistle of Manichaeus,* (JehuBooks. A.D. 397, Kindle edition), Kindle location 89, Chapter 5. Also in the print edition of *Against the Epistle of Manichaeus Called Fundamental* by CreateSpace Independent Publishing Platform, June 7, 2015, p. 13.

11. Augustine and Chrysostom, Edited by Philip Schaff, *Nicene and Post-Nicene Fathers*, Volume 1-14 (Ephesians Four Group, 2015 edition, Kindle edition), Kindle location, 106761.

12. John Calvin, *Commentary on the Book of Psalms* (Amazon Digital Services LLC, 2011 edition, Kindle Edition), Kindle locations 939-943.

13. Dave Hunt, *What Love Is This?* (Bend, OR: The Berean Call, 2013, 4th edition), p. 42. Hunt writes: "Most of those

today, including evangelical leaders who hold Calvin in great esteem, are not aware that they have been captivated by the writings of a devout Roman Catholic, newly converted to Luther's Protestantism, who had broken with Rome only a year before. Oddly, Calvin kept himself on the payroll of the Roman Catholic Church for nearly a year after he claimed to have been miraculously delivered from the "deep slough" of "obstinate addiction to the superstitions of the papacy."

CHAPTER 2: JOHN CALVIN'S MANNER OF LIFE

1. Bernard Cottret, *Calvin: A Biography* (Grand Rapids, MI: Eerdmans Pub. Company, English translation, 2000), p. 181. 2. To read more about Gruet's execution and other Calvin-era executions, read Preserved Smith's (1880-1941) *The Age of the Reformtaion* (New York, NY: Henry Holt and Company, 1920); see page 120 for information about Gruet.

3. J. M. Robertson, *A Short History of Freethought, Ancient and Modern,* Vol. I (London: Owlfoot Press, 1914), p. 352; citing partly from: "Stähelin, i, 400. Henry avows that Gruet was 'subjected to the torture morning and evening during a whole month' (Eng. tr. ii. 66). Other biographers dishonestly exclude the fact from their narratives."

4. "The Murder of Michael Servetus" (http://www.bcbsr.com/topics/servetus.html). Also see *The Ridpath Library of Universal Literature,* Vol. 5, p. 89 by John Clark Ridpath documenting actual letters from Calvin discussing the fate of Servetus.

5. J. M. Robertson, *A Short History of Freethought, Ancient and Modern,* Vol. I, op. cit., p. 354.

6. Will Durant, *The Story of Civilization: The Reformation,* Vol. VI (New York, NY: Simon & Schuster, 1957), pp. 482-484.

7. Dave Hunt, *What Love is This?,* op. cit., p. 79.

8. Brenda Nickel, featured in the documentary film, *Wide is the Gate,* Vol. 2 (Produced by Caryl Productions; available through Lighthouse Trails or The Berean Call; trailer for the film: http://www.lighthousetrails.com/home/29-wide-is-the-gate-dvd-volume-2-the-emerging-new-christianity.html). Her online book on Calvinism, which includes biography on her years as a Calvinist, can be accessed at www.CalvinismNo-More.com.

9. Bernard Cottret, *Calvin: A Biography,* op. cit., p. 208.

10. Dave Hunt, *What Love Is This?,* op. cit., p. 74; partly citing Williston Walker from *John Calvin: The Organizer of Reformed Protestantism* (New York, NY: Schocken Books, 1969), pp. 259 and 107.

11. Ibid., p. 72.

CHAPTER 3: CHANGING THE MEANING OF WORDS

1. "Arthur Pink," Wikipedia, https://en.wikipedia.org/wiki/Arthur_Pink.

2. A. W. Pink, *The Sovereignty of God* (Blacksburg, VA: Wilder Publications, 2008), p. 160.

3. Ibid., p. 163.

4. M.G. Easton, *Illustrated Bible Dictionary* (New York, NY: Harper & Brothers, 1893, Scholar Select scanned edition), p. 641.

5. A. W. Pink, *The Sovereignty of God,* op. cit., p. 163.

6. Ibid., p. 82.

7. Ibid.

8. Gordon H. Clark, *Predestination* (Phillipsburg, NJ: Presbyterian and Reformed Publishing, 1987), p. 102.

9. A.W. Pink, *The Sovereignty of God,* op. cit., p. 113.

10. Arthur Custance, *The Sovereignty of Grace* (P & R Press; First Edition, 1979), p. 18; also at: http://www.custance.org/Library/SOG/Part_I/Chapter2.html#Page5.

11. A.W. Pink, *The Sovereignty of God*, op. cit., p. 57.

12. Sam Storms, *Chosen for Life: The Case for Divine Election* (Wheaton, IL: Crossway Books, a ministry of Good News Publishers, revised and expanded edition, 2007), p. 77.

13. Herman Hoeksema, *Whosoever Will* (Grand Rapids, MI: Eerdman's Publishing Company, First Edition 1945, reprinted 1973), p. 14.

14. Kenneth Talbot and Gary Crampton, *Calvinism, Hyper-Calvinism and Arminianism* (Lakeland, FL: Whitefield Media Publishing, 3rd Edition, 1990), p. 40.

15. A.W. Pink, *The Sovereignty of God*, op. cit., p. 120.

WHAT IS TULIP?

1. Dave Hunt, *T.U.L.I.P. and the Bible: Comparing the Works of Calvin With the Word of God* (Bend, OR: The Berean Call, 2012), p. 146.

2. Ibid., p. 171.

CHAPTER 4: USING A FOOLISH ANALOGY

1. John Calvin, *Concerning the Eternal Predestination of God*, op. cit., p. 63.

CHAPTER 5: CREATED TO CHOOSE AND TO REASON

1. A.W. Pink, *The Sovereignty of God*, op. cit., p. 113.

2. Lorraine Boettner, *The Reformed Doctrine of Predestination* (Phillipsburg, NJ: Presbyterian and Reformed Publishing Company, 1932, 14th printing), page 101, citing Augustine.

3. John Calvin, *Institutes of the Christian Religion,* Vol. 3, op. cit., chapter 21, section 5, Kindle location 17221.

4. Charles H. Spurgeon, "Christ's First and Last Subject" (Sermon #329, https://www.spurgeon.org/resource-library/ sermons/christs-first-and-last-subject#flipbook). While Spurgeon was a Calvinist and held strongly to the "doctrine of election," one can see, by reading his sermons, the conflict he apparently had with Scriptures that clearly refute Calvinism. As Dave Hunt said, "[Spurgeon] was torn between his evangelist's heart that desired the salvation of all and his Calvinistic beliefs. . . . Sometimes he seemed to contradict himself almost within the same breath." Dave Hunt, *What Love is This?, op. cit.*, pp. 19-20, partly citing Spurgeon's "Number One Thousand; Or, 'Bread Enough and to Spare,'" http://www.blueletterbible.org/ Comm/charles_spurgeon/sermons/1000.html).

CHAPTER 7: CALVINISM'S PERSEVERANCE

1. *The American Heritage Dictionary of the English Language* (Boston, MA: Houghton Mifflin Company, 1981 edition), p. 978.

2. John Calvin, *Calvin's Calvinism: God's Eternal Predestination and Secret Providence* (Reformed Free Publishing Association, Kindle edition from the 2009 2nd edition), Kindle location 532.

3. John Calvin, *The First Epistle of Paul the Apostle to the Corinthians* (Grand Rapids, MI: Eerdmans Publishing Company, 1960), p. 197.

4. A.W. Pink, *Practical Christianity* (Zeeland, MI: Reformed Church Publications, 2009), p. 16.

5. A. W. Pink in December 1947, cited in Iain H. Murray's *The Life of Arthur W. Pink* (Carlisle, PA: The Banner of Truth Trust, 1981 edition), pp. 248-249.

6. John Otis, "Who is the Genuine Christian?" (The Counsel of Chalcedon, 1988), p. 20; article on file with publisher.

7. A. W. Pink, *The Doctrine of Sanctification* (Prisbrary Publishing, Kindle edition, Arthur Pink Collection Book 16), Kindle location 374, citing Puritan Walter Marshall, 1692. This book is also available on Amazon in a print edition published by CreateSpace Independent Publishing Platform, July 9, 2016, and the quote is found on page 27.

8. John Murray, *Redemption Accomplished and Applied* (Grand Rapids, MI: Eerdmans Publishing Co. 2015 edition), p. 164.

CHAPTER 8: NO ASSURANCE OF SALVATION

1. Norman F. Douty, *The Death of Christ* (Irving, TX: Williams & Watrous Pub. Co., Revised and Enlarged Edition, 1978), p. 176, citing John Calvin from F. F. Bruce's "Answers and Questions," Questions 1331, in *The Harvester* (Exeter) January 1966.

2. John Murray, *Redemption Accomplished and Applied*, op. cit.

3. Charles Hodge, *A Commentary on the Epistle to the Romans* (Grand Rapids, MI: Eerdman's Publishing, 1983 edition), p. 292.

4. John Murray, *Redemption Accomplished and Applied*, op. cit., p. 165.

5. Philip F. Congdon, "Soteriological Implications of Five-Point Calvinism" (*Journal of the Grace Evangelical Society*, Autumn 1995, Volume 8 | No. 15, https://faithalone.org/wp-content/uploads/1995/09/Journal-of-the-Grace-Evangelical-Society-Vol.8-Autumn-1995-No.15small.pdf), p. 63.

6. R. C. Sproul, "Assurance of Salvation" (Tabletalk, Ligonier Ministries, Inc., 1989), p. 20; cited in Dave Hunt's book, *What Love is This?*, op. cit., from chapter 29, endnote #25.

7. Ibid.

8. John Calvin, *Calvin's Calvinism*, op. cit., Kindle location 3796.

9. John Calvin, *Institutes of the Christian Religion*, op., cit., Kindle location 17793.

10. Edwin H. Palmer, *The Five Points of Calvinism* (Grand Rapids, MI: Baker Books, Enlarged Edition, 1980, 24th printing, 2005), pp. 25, 102.

11. Loraine Boettner, *The Reformed Doctrine of Predestination,* op, cit., p. 32.

12. R.C. Sproul Jr., *Almighty Over All* (Grand Rapids, MI: Baker Books, 1999, Second printing, July 1999), pp. 53-54.

13. A. W. Pink, *The Sovereignty of God,* op. cit., p. 201.

CHAPTER 9: THINK IT THROUGH!

1. John Calvin, *Calvin's Calvinism*, op. cit., Kindle location 3796.

2. Hunt, Dave. *What Love is This?*, op. cit., p. 29.

APPENDIX I: SHOULD CHRISTIANS EXPOSE ERROR?

1. Henry Allen "Harry" Ironside (October 14, 1876—January 15, 1951) was a Canadian-American Bible teacher, preacher, theologian, pastor, and author. You may read more articles by him at www.harryironside.com. His writings are in the public domain. Lighthouse Trails has published a number of his writings.

APPENDIX II: A BIBLICAL PERSPECTIVE ON SALVATION

1. See endnote #2, Introduction.

APPENDIX III: A BIBLICAL PERSPECTIVE ON CONTENDING FOR THE FAITH

1. This appendix is from the booklet *Three Vital Questions on Navigating Discernment* written by Harry Ironside, Paul Proctor, and the editors at Lighthouse Trails (available at www.lighthoustrails.com).

SCRIPTURE INDEX

Numbers

1 Corinthians 1:2 . . . 76
1 Corinthians 1:21 . . . 67
1 Corinthians 5:13 . . . 76
1 Corinthians 11:1 . . . 22
1 Corinthians 16:16 . . . 49
1 John 1:5 . . . 84
1 John 2:2 . . . 30, 62, 64
1 John 2:25 . . . 82
1 John 4:14 . . . 64
1 John 5:1 . . . 102
1 John 5:10 . . . 67
1 John 5:11 . . . 82
1 John 5:13 . . . 56, 82, 102
1 Kings 11:4 . . . 75
1 Kings 16:25 . . . 32
1 Peter 2:13 . . . 49
1 Peter 5:5 . . . 49
1 Samuel 2:25 . . . 49
1 Samuel 8:19 . . . 66
1 Timothy 2:4 . . . 58, 69
1 Timothy 2:6 . . . 63, 69
1 Timothy 4:12 . . . 105
2 Chronicles 7:14 . . . 76
2 John 1: 9-11 . . . 107
2 John 1:9-11 . . . 104
2 Kings 17:15 . . . 51
2 Kings 21:9 . . . 50

2 Peter 2:1-2 . . . 106
2 Peter 3:9 . . . 41, 58, 61
2 Samuel 13:2 . . . 85
2 Thessalonians 2:12 . . . 72
2 Thessalonians 3:14-15 . . . 9, 76, 87
2 Timothy 2:15 . . . 88

A

Acts 4:12 . . . 69
Acts 5:31 . . . 29
Acts 7:51 . . . 70
Acts 7:60 . . . 23
Acts 9:26 . . . 72
Acts 10:34 . . . 58, 69, 99
Acts 11:18 . . . 41
Acts 16:30 . . . 36, 100
Acts 16:31 . . . 100
Acts 17:5 . . . 68, 72
Acts 17:11 . . . 95
Acts 17:30 . . . 28, 40, 62
Acts 18:4 . . . 51
Acts 19:9 . . . 68, 72
Acts 20:29-31 . . . 92
Acts 24:25 . . . 51
Acts 28:24 . . . 68, 72
Acts 28:29 . . . 51

C

Colossians 3:18 . . . 49

Colossians 3:25 . . . 99

D
Deuteronomy 5:21 . . . 85
Deuteronomy 9:12 . . . 52
Deuteronomy 17:3 . . . 52

E
Ephesians 1:3-4 . . . 59
Ephesians 1:4 . . . 57
Ephesians 1:5 . . . 68, 69
Ephesians 2:1 . . . 32, 35, 46
Ephesians 2:1-4 . . . 32
Ephesians 4:1-2 . . . 105
Ephesians 4:14-15 . . . 105
Ephesians 4:25 . . . 105
Ephesians 4:28 . . . 53
Ephesians 4:29 . . . 105
Ephesians 5:22 . . . 49
Ephesians 6:9 . . . 99
Ephesians 6:18 . . . 73
Exodus 6:9 . . . 49
Exodus 16:20 . . . 49
Exodus 20:3 . . . 52
Exodus 20:4 . . . 52
Exodus 20:7 . . . 52
Exodus 20:8 . . . 52
Exodus 20:12 . . . 52
Exodus 20:13 . . . 53
Exodus 20:14 . . . 53
Exodus 20:15 . . . 53
Exodus 20:16 . . . 53

Exodus 20:17 . . . 53
Ezekiel 33:11-13 . . . 98
Ezekiel 16:47 . . . 32
Ezekiel 33:17-20 . . . 98
Ezekiel 33:1,7 . . . 98
Ezra 8:22 . . . 30

G
Galatians 1:6-10 . . . 108
Galatians 2: 4-5 . . . 108
Galatians 2:16, 21 . . . 77
Galatians 3:8 . . . 28
Galatians 5:7 . . . 87
Galatians 5:9 . . . 94
Galatians 5:19-21 . . . 107
Galatians 5:22 . . . 24
Genesis 1:26 . . . 43
Genesis 2:15-17 . . . 44
Genesis 2:17 . . . 35
Genesis 3:6 . . . 44
Genesis 3:11 . . . 45
Genesis 3: 22-24 . . . 46
Genesis 12:3 . . . 48
Genesis 19:5 . . . 85
Genesis 37:35 . . . 66

H
Hebrews 4:12 . . . 103
Hebrews 10:39 . . . 67
Hebrews 11:1 . . . 56
Hebrews 11:24 . . . 66
Hebrews 11:25 . . . 64
Hebrews 11:31 . . . 72

Hebrews 12:25 . . . 66
Hebrews 13:13 . . . 94
Hebrews 13:17 . . . 49
Hosea 4:6 . . . 51

I

Isaiah 1:18 . . . 36, 50
Isaiah 30:21 . . . 51
Isaiah 47:10 . . . 49

J

James 1:3 . . . 45
James 4:7 . . . 49
Jeremiah 7:24 . . . 50
Jeremiah 7:26 . . . 32, 50
Jeremiah 11:9-10 . . . 66
Jeremiah 13:25 . . . 49
Jeremiah 23:14 . . . 53
Jeremiah 36:31 . . . 50
Jeremiah 48:7 . . . 49
Jeremiah 49:4 . . . 49
John 1:12 . . . 66
John 1:29 . . . 63
John 3:15 . . . 42
John 3:16 . . . 25-28, 42, 63
John 3:17 . . . 63
John 3:18 . . . 67
John 3:36 . . . 42, 79
John 4:48 . . . 39
John 5:24 . . . 42
John 5:40 . . . 39, 41, 71
John 6:35 . . . 96
John 6:40 . . . 42

John 6:44 . . . 39
John 6:55,57 . . . 96
John 6:58 . . . 96
John 6:62 . . . 96
John 6:63 . . . 96
John 6:64 . . . 72
John 6:68 . . . 82
John 9:35-38 . . . 38
John 10:25 . . . 72
John 12:32 . . . 40, 61
John 12:37 . . . 68, 72
John 13:15 . . . 22
John 15:16 . . . 58
John 15:18-19 . . . 27
John 20:31 . . . 38, 42, 67
Joshua 6:3 . . . 28
Joshua 7:21 . . . 53
Joshua 24:15 . . . 65
Jude 1:3 . . . 88, 92
Jude 1:3-4 . . . 92-93
Jude 1:3-5 . . . 107-108
Jude 1:5 . . . 72
Jude 1:17-23 . . . 106
Judges 2:19 . . . 32

L

Leviticus 20:7 . . . 52
Luke 3:16 . . . 100
Luke 7:28 . . . 100
Luke 8:50, 55 . . . 38
Luke 10:3-12 . . . 109
Luke 13:3 . . . 26, 40

Luke 13:27 . . . 28
Luke 14: 23 . . . 14
Luke 18:42-43 . . . 37
Luke 20:5 . . . 50
Luke 20:14 . . . 50
Luke 22:19 . . . 96
Luke 23:34 . . . 22

M

Mark 1:2,4 . . . 100
Mark 2:6 . . . 51
Mark 2:8 . . . 50
Mark 7:9 . . . 51
Mark 8:16 . . . 50
Mark 9:23-24 . . . 37
Mark 11:31 . . . 50
Matthew 5:44 . . . 22
Matthew 7:15 . . . 105
Matthew 8:10, 13 . . . 36
Matthew 9:21-22 . . . 37
Matthew 9:28-30 . . . 37
Matthew 10:21 . . . 53
Matthew 15:28 . . . 37
Matthew 23:37 . . . 39

N

Nehemiah 9:17 . . . 65
Nehemiah 13:17 . . . 52
Numbers 14:18 . . . 70

P

Proverbs 1:24 . . . 66,
    70-71

Proverbs 1:29 . . . 65
Proverbs 11:30 . . . 58
Proverbs 29:1 . . . 71
Psalm 4:5 . . . 48
Psalm 10:4 . . . 31
Psalm 11:6 . . . 31
Psalm 13:5 . . . 31
Psalm 27:12 . . . 53
Psalm 31:23 . . . 28
Psalm 31:24 . . . 28
Psalm 32:11 . . . 28
Psalm 37:3 . . . 48
Psalm 78:10 . . . 65, 66
Psalm 78:22 . . . 48, 67
Psalm 78:32 . . . 67
Psalm 78:58 . . . 52
Psalm 81:12 . . . 51
Psalm 94:6 . . . 53
Psalm 103:8 . . . 70
Psalm 106:24 . . . 67, 72
Psalm 134:1 . . . 28
Psalm 139:20 . . . 52

R

Revelation 2: 2-3 . . . 108
Revelation 19:5 . . . 28
Revelation 22:13 . . . 60
Revelation 22:17 . . . 40,
    58, 60, 102
Romans 1: 19-20 . . . 32
Romans 1:30 . . . 85
Romans 2:11 . . . 99

Romans 3:8 . . . 84
Romans 5:1 . . . 82
Romans 5:12 . . . 28, 61
Romans 8:29 . . . 59
Romans 8:29-30 . . . 59
Romans 10:13 . . . 61
Romans 13:12 . . . 104
Romans 14:11-12 . . . 40
Romans 15:14 . . . 9
Romans 16:17 . . . 88

T

Titus 1:2 . . . 45
Titus 2:11 . . . 61
Titus 3:10 . . . 9, 87
Titus 3:10-11 . . . 106

Z

Zechariah 2:8 . . . 48
Zechariah 7:11 . . . 66
Zechariah 11:12-13 . . . 48

What Love Is This?

An In-depth study on Calvinism by Dave Hunt

Discussions with many people around the world reveal that multitudes of sincere, Bible-believing Christians are "Calvinists" only by default. It takes only a few simple questions to discover the fact that most of those who regard themselves as Calvinists are largely unaware of what John Calvin and his early followers of the sixteenth and seventeenth centuries actually believed and practiced. Nor do they fully understand what most of today's leading Calvinists believe. *What Love Is This?* exposes the true beliefs of Calvinism and addresses all the issues surrounding this doctrine.

Published by The Berean Call | Available through TBC, Lighthouse Trails, or most major book outlets. Retail $23.95 | 546 pages, 4th Edition

SOME OF THE TOPICS THIS BOOK ADDRESSES:

- Is Biblical Understanding Reserved for an Elite?
- John Calvin and His Institutes
- Calvinism's Surprising Catholic Connection
- Irresistibly Imposed "Christianity"
- Arminius, Dort, Westminster, and Five Points
- Total Depravity
- The Solemn Issue: God's Character
- The Truth about Human Depravity
- A Distorted Sovereignty
- Sovereignty and Free Will

- Foreknowledge and Man's Will
- Erasmus and Luther in Debate
- The Bondage of the Will?
- Unconditional Election
- Is Salvation Available to All?
- Foreknowledge and Predestination/Election
- Limited Atonement
- Abusing God's Word
- Irresistible Grace
- When Grace Isn't Grace
- Grace and Human Responsibility
- Calvinism's Errors Are Serious
- Persuasion, the Gospel, and God
- When Is "Love" Not Love?
- Perseverance of the Saints

An Urgent Message to the Last-Days Church

THE GOOD SHEPHERD CALLS

BY ROGER OAKLAND

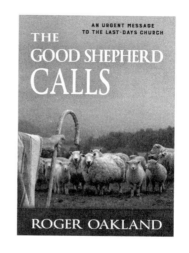

SINCE THE TURN of the millennium, in particular since September 11, 2001 when America was attacked by terrorists triggering a global-wide spiritual paradigm shift, Christianity as we have known it has experienced a major meltdown. While many are saying Christianity is on the brink of a great revival and even a "new reformation," in reality, we are witnessing the greatest apostasy in modern-day history.

The Good Shepherd Calls brings clarity to what this delusion looks like, why it is happening, where it is headed, and what can still be done to warn believers and unbelievers alike.

| \$14.95 | 288 pages | Quantity discounts available Available from Lighthouse Trails or most online book outlets or walk-in bookstores.

OTHER BOOKS BY LIGHTHOUSE TRAILS

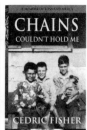

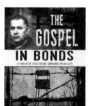

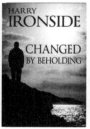

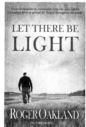

For a complete listing of all Lighthouse Trails books, booklets, DVDs, CDs, and more, request a catalog by calling or writing, or visit our website at www.lighthousetrails.com.

To order additional copies of:
Calvin: None Dare Call It Heresy
Send $11.95 per book plus shipping to:
Lighthouse Trails Publishing
P.O. Box 908
Eureka, MT 59917
(U.S. Shipping is $3.50 for 1 book;
$5.25/2-3 books; $10.95/4-20 books)

You may also purchase Lighthouse Trails books from
www.lighthousetrails.com. For a complete listing of all
Lighthouse Trails resources, request a free catalog.

For bulk rates of 10 or more copies (40% off retail), contact
Lighthouse Trails Publishing, either by phone, e-mail, or
fax. You may also order retail or bulk online at www.light-
housetrails.com, or call our toll-free number:
866/876-3910 (USA/CA)
For international and all other calls:
406/889-3610
Fax: 406/889-3633

Calvinism: None Dare Call It Heresy, as well as other books by
Lighthouse Trails Publishing, can be ordered through all major outlet stores, bookstores, online bookstores, and Christian
bookstores in the U.S. Bookstores may order through: In-
gram, SpringArbor, Anchor, or directly through Lighthouse
Trails. Libraries may order through Baker & Taylor.

Visit our research site at www.lighthousetrailsresearch.com.